The triumph

perseverance and e

Recorded as examples for the young

Thomas Cooper

Alpha Editions

This edition published in 2024

ISBN : 9789362094971

Design and Setting By
Alpha Editions
www.alphaedis.com
Email - info@alphaedis.com

Contents

PREFACE.

These records of the Triumphs of Perseverance and Enterprise have been written with the view to inspire the youthful reader with a glow of emulation, and to induce him to toil and to advance in the peaceful achievements of science and benevolence, remembering the adage, "Whatever man has done, man may do."

CHAPTER I.
LINGUISTS.

SIR WILLIAM JONES.—DR. SAMUEL LEE.

"If that boy were left naked and friendless on Salisbury Plain, he would find the road to fame and riches!" the tutor of SIR WILLIAM JONES was accustomed to say of his illustrious pupil. His observation of the great quality of *perseverance*, evinced in every act of study prescribed to his scholar, doubtless impelled the teacher to utter that remarkable affirmation. A discernment of high genius in young Jones, with but little of the great quality we have named, would have led Dr. Thackeray to modify his remark. It would have been couched in some such form as this: "If that boy had as much perseverance as genius, he would find the road to fame and riches, even if he were left naked and friendless on Salisbury Plain." But, had the instructor regarded his pupil as one endowed with the most brilliant powers of mind, yet entirely destitute of perseverance, he would have pronounced a judgment very widely different from the first. "Alas, for this boy!" he might have said, "how will these shining qualities, fitfully bursting forth in his wayward course through life, displaying their lustre in a thousand beginnings which will lead to nothing, leave him to be regarded as an object of derision where he might have won general admiration and esteem, and cast him for subsistence on the bounty or pity of others, when he might have been a noble example of self-dependence!"

Let the reflection we would awaken by these introductory sentences be of a healthy character. It is not meant that celebrity or wealth are the most desirable rewards of a well-spent life; but that the most resplendent natural powers, unless combined with application and industry, fail to bring happiness to the heart and mind of the possessor, or to render him useful to his brother men. It is sought to impress deeply and enduringly on the youthful understanding, the irrefragable truth that, while genius is a gift which none can create for himself, and may be uselessly possessed, perseverance has enabled many, who were born with only ordinary faculties of imagination, judgment, and memory, to attain a first-rate position in literature or science, or in the direction of human affairs, and to leave a perpetual name in the list of the world's benefactors.

Has the youthful reader formed a purpose for life? We ask not whether he has conceived a vulgar passion for fame or riches, but earnestly exhort him to self-enquiry, whether he be wasting existence in what is termed amusement, or be daily devoting the moments at his command to a diligent preparation for usefulness? Whether he has hitherto viewed life as a journey to be trod without aims and ends, or a grand field of enterprise in which it is both his duty and interest to become an industrious and honourable worker? Has he found, by personal experience, even in the outset of life, that time spent in purposeless inactivity or frivolity produces no results on which the mind can dwell with satisfaction? And has he learned, from the testimony of others, that years so misspent bring only a feeling of self-accusation, which increases in bitterness as the loiterer becomes older, and the possibility of "redeeming the time" becomes more doubtful? Did he ever reflect that indolence never yet led to real distinction; that sloth never yet opened the path to independence; that trifling never yet enabled a man to make useful or solid acquirements?

If such reflections have already found a place in the reader's mind, and created in him some degree of yearning to make his life not only a monument of independence, but of usefulness, we invite him to a rapid review of the lives of men among whom he will not only find the highest exemplars of perseverance, but some whose peculiar difficulties may resemble his own, and whose triumphs may encourage him to pursue a course of similar excellence. Purposing to awaken the spirit of exertion by the presentation of striking examples rather than the rehearsal of formal precepts, we proceed to open our condensed chronicle with a notice of the universal scholar just named, and whose world-famed career has entitled him to a first place in the records of the "Triumphs of Perseverance."

SIR WILLIAM JONES,

Happily, had early admonitions of perseverance from his mother, in whose widowed care he was left at three years old; and who, "to his incessant importunities for information, which she watchfully stimulated," says his biographer, Lord Teignmouth, "perpetually answered, 'Read, and you will know,'" His earnest mind cleaved to the injunction. He could read any English book rapidly at four years of age; and, though his right eye was injured by an accident at five, and the sight of it ever remained imperfect, his determination to learn triumphed over that impediment. Again, the commencement of life seemed discouraging: he had been placed at Harrow School, at the age of seven, but had his thigh-bone broken at nine, and was compelled to be from school for twelve months. Such was his progress, in spite of these untoward circumstances, and although characterised, let it be especially observed, as a boy "remarkable for diligence and application rather than superiority of talent," that he was removed into the upper school, at Harrow, in his twelfth year. At this period he is found writing out the entire play of the "Tempest," from memory, his companions intending to perform it, and not having a copy in their possession. Virgil's Pastorals and Ovid's Epistles are, at the same age, turned into melodious English verse by him; he has learned the Greek characters for his amusement, and now applies himself to the language in earnest; his mother has taught him drawing, during the vacations; and he next composes a drama, on the classic story of "Meleager," which is acted in the school. During the next two years he "wrote out the exercises of many of the boys in the upper classes, and they were glad to become his pupils;" meanwhile, in the holidays, he learned French and arithmetic.

But this early and unremitting tension of the mind, did it not leave the heart uncultured? Were not pride and overweening growing within, and did not sourness of temper display itself, and repel some whom the young scholar's acquirements might otherwise have attached to him? Ah! youthful reader, thou wilt never find any so proud as the ignorant; and, if thou wouldst not have thy heart become a garden of rank and pestilential weeds, leave not the key thereof in the soft hand of Indolence, but entrust it to the sinewed grasp of Industry. What testimony give his early companions to the temper and hearing of young Jones? The celebrated Dr. Parr—in his own person also a high exemplar of the virtue we are inculcating—was his playmate in boyhood, remained his ardent friend in manhood, and never spoke of their early attachment without deep feeling. Dr. Bennet, afterwards Bishop of Cloyne, thus speaks of Sir William Jones: "I knew him from the early age of eight or nine, and he was always an uncommon boy. I loved him and revered him: and, though one or two years older than he was, was always instructed by him." ... "In a word, I can only say of this amiable and wonderful man, that he had more virtues and less faults than I ever yet saw in any human being; and that the goodness of his head, admirable as it was, was exceeded by that of his heart."

With the boys, generally, he was a favourite. Dr. Sumner, who succeeded Dr. Thackeray, used to say Jones knew more Greek than himself. He soon learned the Arabic characters, and was already able to read Hebrew. A mere stripling, yet he would devote whole nights to study, taking coffee or tea as an antidote to drowsiness. Strangers were accustomed to enquire for him, at the school, under the title of "the great scholar." But Dr. Sumner, during the last months spent at Harrow, was obliged to interdict the juvenile "great scholar's" application, in consequence of a returning weakness in his injured eye: yet he continued to compose, and dictated to younger students; alternately practising the games of Philidor and acquiring a knowledge of chess. He had added a knowledge of botany and fossils to the acquirements already mentioned, and had learned Italian during his last vacation.

Let us mark, again, whether all this ardent intellectual activity cramps the right growth of the affections, and warps the heart's sense of filial duty. "His mother," says his excellent biographer, "allowed him unlimited credit on her purse; but of this indulgence, as he knew her finances were restricted, he availed himself no further than to purchase such books as were essential to his improvement." And when he is removed, at the age of seventeen, to University College, Oxford, he is not anxious to enter the world without restraint; his mother goes to reside at Oxford, "at her son's request." And how he toiled, and wished for college honours, not for vain distinction, not for love of gain, but from the healthy growth of that filial affection, which had strengthened with his judgment and power of reflection! He "anxiously wished for a fellowship," says Lord Teignmouth, "to enable him to draw less frequently upon his mother, knowing the contracted nature of her income." His heart was soon to be gratified.

He commenced Arabic zealously, soon after reaching the University; he perused, with assiduity, all the Greek poets and historians of note; he read the entire works of Plato and Lucian, with commentaries, constantly ready, with a pen in his hand, to make any remark that he judged worth preserving. What a contrast to the "reader for amusement," who will leave the priceless treasure of a book ungathered, because it is hid in what he calls a "lumbering folio," and it wearies his hands, or it is inconvenient to read it while lying along at ease on the sofa! Yet this "great scholar" was no mere musty book-worm; he did not claim kindred with Dryasdust. While passing his vacations in London, he daily attended the noted schools of Angelo, and acquired a skill in horsemanship and fencing, as elegant accomplishments; his evenings, at these seasons, being devoted to the perusal of the best Italian, Spanish, and Portuguese writers. At the University, how was the stripling urging his way into the regions of oriental learning—that grand high-road of his fame that was to be! He had found Mirza, a Syrian, who possessed a knowledge of the vernacular Arabic, and spent some portion of every morning in writing out a translation of Galland's French version of the Arabian Tales into Arabic, from the mouth of the Syrian; and he then corrected the grammatical inaccuracies by the help of lexicons. From the Arabic he urged his way into the Persian, becoming soon enraptured with that most elegant of all eastern languages. Such was this true disciple of "Perseverance" at the age of *nineteen*.

And now some measure of the rewards of industry, honour, and virtue begin to alight upon him. He is appointed tutor to Lord Althorpe, son of the literary Earl Spencer; finds his pupil possessed of a mind and disposition that will render his office delightful; has the range of one of the most splendid private libraries in the kingdom, together with the refined and agreeable society of Wimbledon Park; and is presented, soon after, with a fellowship by his college.

Mark well, from two incidents which occur about this time, what high conscientiousness, deep modesty, and sterling independence characterise the true scholar. The Duke of Grafton, then premier, offered him the situation of government interpreter for eastern languages. He declined it, recommending the Syrian, Mirza, as one better qualified to fill it than himself. His recommendation was neglected; and his biographer remarks that "a better knowledge of the world would have led him to accept the office, and to convey the emoluments to his friend Mirza. He was too ingenuous to do so. He saw the excellent lady who afterwards became his wife and devoted companion in study; but 'his fixed idea of an honourable independence, and a determined resolution never to owe his fortune to a wife, or her kindred, excluded all ideas of a matrimonial connection,'" at that period, although the affection he had conceived was ardent.

In the year of his majority, we find him commencing his famous "Commentaries on Asiatic Poetry;" copying the keys of the Chinese language; learning German, by conversation, grammar, and dictionary, during three weeks passed at Spa with his noble pupil; acquiring a knowledge of the broad-sword exercise from an old pensioner at Chelsea; continuing to attend the two schools of Signor Angelo; and secretly taking lessons in dancing from Gallini, the dancing-master of Earl Spencer's family, until he surprises the elegant inhabitants of Wimbledon by joining with grace in the amusements of their evening parties.

Such was the truly magnificent advancement made by this illustrious disciple of "Perseverance," up to the age of twenty-one. Think, reader, how much may be done in the opening of life! How elevated the course of Sir William Jones! What cheering self-approval must he have experienced, in looking back on the youthful years thus industriously spent; but what humbling reflection, what severe self-laceration would he have felt, had he allowed indolence to master him, ease to enervate him, listlessness and dissipation to render him a nameless and worthless nothing in the world!

At the close of his twenty-first year he peruses the little treatise of our ancient lawyer, Fortescue, in praise of the laws of England. His large learning enabled him to compare the laws of other countries with his own; and though he had, hitherto, enthusiastically preferred the laws of republican Greece, reflection, on the perusal of this treatise, led him to prefer the laws of England to all others. His noble biographer adds a remark which indicates the solidity and perspicacity of Sir William Jones's judgment:—"He was not, however, regardless of the deviations in practice from the theoretical perfection of the constitution, in a contested election, of which he was an unwilling spectator." Yet the perfect *theory* of our constitution so far attracted him, as to lead him, from this time, to the resolve of uniting the study of the law to his great philological acquirements; his purpose was neither rashly formed, nor soon relinquished, like the miscalled "purposes" of weak men and idlers; it resulted in his elevation to high and honourable usefulness, in the lapse of a few years.

In his twenty-second year the "great scholar" undertakes a task which no other quality than perseverance could have enabled him to accomplish. The King of Denmark, then on a visit to this country, brought over with him an eastern manuscript, containing a life of Nadir Shah, and expressed his wish to the officers of government to have it translated into French, by an English scholar. The under secretary of state applied to Sir William Jones, who recommended Major Dow, the able translator of a Persian history, to perform the work. Major Dow refused: and, though hints of greater patronage did not influence the inclination of Sir William Jones, his reflection that the reputation of English learning would be dishonoured by the Danish king taking back the manuscript, with a report that no scholar in our country had courage to undertake the difficult labour, impelled him to enter on it. The fact that he had a French style to acquire, in order to discharge his task, and had, even then, to get a native Frenchman to go over the translation, to render it a scholar-like production, made the undertaking extremely arduous. It was, however, accomplished magnificently; and the adventurous translator added a treatise on oriental poetry, "such as no other person in England could then have written." He was immediately afterwards made a member of the Royal Society of Copenhagen, and was recommended by the King of Denmark to the particular patronage of his own sovereign.

At twenty-six he was made a fellow of the Royal Society of England, and took his degree of Master of Arts the year after. Meanwhile he was composing his celebrated Persian Grammar; had found the means of entering effectively on the study of Chinese, a language at that time surrounded with unspeakable difficulties; had written part of a Turkish history; and was assiduously copying Arabic manuscripts in the Bodleian. The "Commentaries on Asiatic Poetry" were published in his twenty-eighth year, being five years after they were finished; his modesty, that invariable attendant of true merit, and his love of correctness, having induced him to lay the manuscript before Dr. Parr, and other profound judges, ere he ventured to give his composition to the world. Amidst so many absorbing engagements his biographer still notes the correct state of his heart. He was a regular correspondent with his excellent mother, and ever paid the most affectionate attention to her and his sister.

In his twenty-eighth year he devotes himself more exclusively to his legal studies, goes the Oxford circuit after being called to the bar, and afterwards attends regularly at Westminster Hall. Except the publication of a translation of the speeches of Isæus, he performs no remarkable literary labour for the next few years; his professional practice having become very considerable, and his thoughts being strongly directed towards a vacant judgeship, at Calcutta, as the situation in which he felt assured, by the union of his legal knowledge with his skill in oriental languages, he could best serve the interests of learning and of mankind.

Before this object of his laudable ambition was attained, however, Sir William Jones gave proof, as our great Englishman, Milton, had given before him, that the mightiest erudition does not narrow, but serves truly to enlarge the mind, and to nourish its sympathies with the great brotherhood of humanity. The war with the United States of America had commenced, and he declared himself against it; he wrote a splendid Latin ode, entitled "Liberty," in which his patriotic and philanthropic sentiments are most nobly embodied; and became a candidate, on what are now called "liberal principles," for the representation of Oxford. He withdrew, after further reflection, from the candidateship, still purposing to devote his life to the East, but not before he had testified his disapproval of harsh ministerial measures, by publishing an "Enquiry into the legal mode of suppressing riots, with a constitutional plan for their suppression." Finally, to the record of this part of his life, Lord Teignmouth adds the relation, that Sir William Jones had found time to attend the lectures of the celebrated John Hunter, and to acquire some knowledge of anatomy; while he had advanced sufficiently far into the mathematics to be able to read and understand the "Principia" of Sir Isaac Newton.

The last eleven years of the illustrious scholar's life form the most brilliant part of his career, and only leave us to lament that his days were not more extended. In the month of March, 1783, being then in his thirty-seventh year, he was appointed a judge of the supreme court of judicature, Fortwilliam, Calcutta, and on that occasion received the honour of knighthood. In the following month he married the eldest daughter of Dr. Shipley, Bishop of St. Asaph, and thus happy in a union with the lady to whom he had been long devoted, almost immediately embarked for India.

As a concluding lesson from the life of Sir William Jones, let us note how unsubduable is the intellect trained by long and early habits of perseverance, under the corrupting and enfeebling influences of honours and prosperity. On the voyage, the "great scholar" drew up a list of "Objects of Enquiry."

If he could have fulfilled the gigantic schemes which were thus unfolding themselves to his ardent mind, the world must have been stricken with amazement. The list is too long to be detailed here; suffice it to say, that it enumerates the "Laws of the Hindus and Mahommedans," "The History of the Ancient World," all the sciences, all the arts and inventions of all the Asiatic nations, and the various kinds of government in India. Following the list of "Objects of Enquiry," is a sketch of works he purposes to write and publish; including "Elements of the Laws of England," "History of the American War," an epic poem, to be entitled "Britain Discovered," "Speeches, Political and Forensic," "Dialogues, Philosophical and Historical," and a volume of letters, with translations of some portions of the Scriptures into Arabic and Persian.

Intense and indefatigable labour enabled him to complete his masterly "Digest of Mahommedan and Hindu Law," but to accomplish this work, so invaluable to the European conquerors of Hindoostan, he had first, critically, to master the Sanscrit, at once the most perfect and most difficult of known languages. If it be remembered that Sir William Jones was also most active in the discharge of his judicial duties, our admiration will be increased. His translation of the "Ordinances of Menu," a Sanscrit work, displaying the Hindoo system of religious and civil duties—and of the Indian drama of "Sacontala," written a century before the Christian era—and his production of a "Dissertation on the Gods of Greece, Italy, and Rome," were among the last of his complete works. He also edited the first volume of the "Asiatic Researches;" and gave an impetus to eastern enquiry among Europeans, by instituting the Asiatic Society, of which he was the first president. His annual discourses before that assembly have been published, and are well known and highly valued.

The death of this great and good man, though sudden, being occasioned by the rapid liver complaint of Bengal, was as peaceful as his life had been noble and virtuous. A friend, who saw him die, says that he expired "without a groan, and with a serene and complacent look." His death took place on the 27th April, 1794, when he was only in his forty-eighth year; yet he had acquired a "critical knowledge" of eight languages—English, Latin, French, Italian, Greek, Arabic, Persian, Sanscrit; he knew eight others less perfectly, but was able to read them with the occasional use of a dictionary—Spanish, Portuguese, German, Runic, Hebrew, Bengalee, Hindostanee, Turkish; and he knew so much of twelve other tongues, that they were perfectly attainable by him, had life and leisure permitted his continued application to them— Tibetian, Pâli, Phalavi, Deri, Russian, Syriac, Ethiopic, Coptic, Welsh, Swedish, Dutch, Chinese. Twenty-eight languages in all; such is his own account. When you sum up the other diversified accomplishments and attainments of the scarce forty-eight years of Sir William Jones, reflect deeply, youthful reader, on what may be achieved by "perseverance," and when you have reflected—*resolve*.

To that emphatic early lesson of "read and you will learn," and to his ready opportunities and means of culture, we must, undoubtedly, attribute much of the "great scholar's" success. In the life of one still living, and enjoying the honours and rewards of virtuous perseverance, it will be seen that even devoid of help, unstimulated by any affectionate voice in the outset, and surrounded with discouragements, almost at every step, the cultivation of this grand quality infallibly leads on to signal triumph.

DR. SAMUEL LEE,

Now Regius Professor of Hebrew in the University of Cambridge, being the son of a poor widow, who was left to struggle for the support of two younger children, was apprenticed to a carpenter, at twelve years of age, after receiving a merely elementary instruction in reading, writing, and arithmetic in the charity-school of the village of Longmore, in Shropshire. His love of books became fervent, and the Latin quotations he found in such as were within his reach kindled a desire to penetrate the mystery of their meaning. The sounds of the language, too, which he heard in a Catholic chapel, where his master had undertaken some repairs, increased this desire. At seventeen he purchased "Ruddiman's Latin Rudiments," and soon committed the whole to memory. With the help of "Corderius' Colloquies," "Entick's Dictionary," and "Beza's Testament," he began to make his way into the vestibule of Roman learning; but of the magnificent inner-glory he had, as yet, scarcely caught a glimpse. The obstacles seemed so great for an unassisted adventurer, that he one day besought a priest of the chapel, where he was still at work, to afford him some help. "Charity begins at home!" was the repelling reply to his application; but, whether meant to indicate the priest's own need of instruction, or sordid unwillingness to afford his help without pecuniary remuneration, does not appear. Unchilled by this repulse, the young and unfriended disciple of "perseverance" girt up "the loins of his mind" for his solitary but onward travel. Yet how uncheering the landscape around him! Think of it, and blush, young reader, if thou art surrounded with ease and comfort, but hast yielded to indolence; ponder on it, and take courage, if thou art the companion of hardship, but resolvest to be a man, one day, amongst men. Young Lee's wages were but six shillings weekly at seventeen years old; and from this small sum he had not only to find food, but to pay for his washing and lodging. The next year his weekly income was increased one shilling, and the year following another. Privation, even of the necessaries of life, he had to suffer, not seldom, in order to enable himself to possess what he desired, now more intensely than ever. He successively purchased a Latin Bible, Cæsar, Justin, Sallust, Cicero, Virgil, Horace, Ovid; having frequently to sell his volume as soon as he had mastered it in order to buy another. But what of that? The true disciple of perseverance looks onward with hope—hope which is not fantastic, but founded in the firmest reason—to the day when his meritorious and ennobling toil shall have its happy fruition, and he shall know no scarcity of books.

Conquest of one language has inspired him with zeal for further victory; it is the genuine nature of enterprise. Freed from his apprenticeship he purchases a Greek grammar, testament, lexicon, and exercises; and soon, the self-taught carpenter, the scholar of toil and privation, holds converse, in their own superlative tongue, with the simple elegance of Xenophon, the eloquence and wisdom of Plato, and the wit of Lucian; he becomes familiar with the glorious "Iliad," with the pathos and refinement, the force and splendour, of the "Antigone," of Sophocles.

"Unaided by any instructor, uncheered by any literary companion," says one who narrates the circumstances of his early career, "he still persevered." What wonder, when he had discovered so much to cheer him in the delectable mental realm he was thus subduing for himself! And he was now endued with the full energy of conquest. He purchased "Bythner's Hebrew Grammar," and "Lyra Prophetica," with a Hebrew Psalter, and was soon able to read the Psalms in the original. Buxtorf's grammar and lexicon with a Hebrew Bible followed; an accident threw in his way the "Targum" of Onkelos, and with the Chaldee grammar in Bythner, and Schindler's lexicon, he was soon able to read it. Another effort, and he was able to read the Syriac Testament and the Samaritan Pentateuch, thus gaining acquaintance with four branches of the ancient Aramœan or Shemitic family of languages, in addition to his knowledge of the two grand Pelasgic dialects.

He was now five-and-twenty, and had mastered six languages, without the slightest help from any living instructor; some of the last-named books were heavily expensive; yet, true to the nobility of life that had distinguished his early youth, he had not relaxed the reins of economy, but had purchased a chest of tools, which had cost him twenty-five pounds.

Suddenly an event befel him which seemed to wither not only his prospects of further mental advancement, but plunged him into the deepest distress. A fire, which broke out in a house he was repairing, consumed his chest of tools; and, as he had no money to purchase more, and had now to feel solicitude for the welfare of an affectionate wife, as well as for himself, his affliction was heavy. In this distracting difficulty he turned his thoughts towards commencing a village school, but even for this he lacked the means of procuring the necessary, though scanty, furniture. Uprightness and meritorious industry, however, seldom fail to attract benevolent help to a man in need. Archdeacon Corbett, the resident philanthropic clergyman of Longmore, heard of Samuel Lee's distress, sent for him, and on hearing the relation of his laudable struggles, used his interest to place him in the mastership of Shrewsbury Charity School, giving him what was of still higher value, an introduction to the great oriental scholar, Dr. Jonathan Scott.

New triumphs succeeded his misfortunes, and a cheering and honourable future was preparing. Dr. Scott put into the hands of his new and humble friend elementary books on Arabic, Persian, and Hindostanee; and, in a few months, the disciple of perseverance was not only able to read and translate, but even essayed to compose in his newly-acquired languages. So effectually had he mastered these eastern tongues, that the good doctor used his influence in introducing him as private tutor to sons of gentlemen going out to India; and, after another brief probation, procured him admission into Queen's College, Cambridge.

Our sketch of this remarkable living scholar may here be cut short. He has made himself master of twenty languages, distinguished himself alike by the virtue of his private life, his practical eloquence in the pulpit and zeal for the church, of which he is an honoured member; and, in addition to the service he has rendered to oriental literature, by his new Hebrew grammar and lexicon, his revision of Sir William Jones's Persian grammar, and a number of philological tracts, has won respect and gratitude, by diligent and laborious supervision of numerous translations of the Scriptures into eastern tongues, prepared by the direction and at the cost of the British and Foreign Bible Society.

If the young scholar be bent on the acquirement of languages, he will find, in the lives of Alexander, Murray, Leyden, Heyne, Carey, Marshman, Morrison, Magliabechi, and a hundred others, striking proofs of the ease with which the mind overcomes all difficulties when it is armed with determination, and never becomes a recreant from the banner of perseverance.

CHAPTER II.
AUTHORS.

SHAKSPEARE.—SPENSER.—JOHNSON.—GIFFORD.—GIBBON.

Creative genius is popularly held to be dependent on faculties widely diverse from those required by the mere man of learning. The linguist is usually regarded as a traveller on a beaten track; the poet, as a discoverer of new regions. Success for the man of learning is considered to depend on diligence in the exercise of the memory and judgment; while obedience to impulse seems to be the mental law popularly allotted to poets. Let the young reader inquire for himself, whether there is not something of fallacy in this popular notion.

SHAKSPEARE,

The most highly endowed of human intelligences, was under as great necessity of learning the vocabulary of the English tongue as the very commonest mind. He, like all other men, however inferior to him in understanding or imagination, was born without any innate knowledge of things, or their natures, words, or the rules for fashioning them in order, or combining them with grace and harmony, eloquence and strength. Every author of the first class was in the same predicament mentally at birth; they had everything to learn, and the perfection of their learning depended on their own effort. It may be equally affirmed, then, of the highest poet and the greatest linguist, of Shakspeare and Sir William Jones, that neither had any "royal road" for gaining his peculiar eminence.

The little we know of the personal history of Shakspeare renders it necessary for us to attribute a very ample measure of his unrivalled excellence to that quality of the mind which we are insisting upon as requisite for the performance of great and exalted labours. If it be true that schoolmasters taught him little, how indefatigable must have been that perseverance which enabled him, not simply to equal, but so immeasurably to transcend his more learned contemporaries and fellow-workers, in the wealth of his language, and in the beauty and fitness of its application! If his helps were few, so much the more astonishing is the energy and continuity of effort which issued in securing for him who exerted it the highest name in the world's literature. Nor can minds of primal order be satisfied with a passing ovation that may be forgotten; they thirst to render their triumphs monumental. Our grand dramatist piled effort upon effort, until he left to the world the priceless legacy of his thirty-seven plays. His mind had none of the sickly quality which views a settled form of composition as irksome, and indulges its unhealthy fantasies in irregular and useless essays. He wrought out his magnificent and self-appointed task to the end; he made his own monument worthy of himself.

Birthplace of Shakspeare.

SPENSER,

Was not less an exemplar of diligence than of skill in the architecture of verse. The mere task-work of constructing three thousand eight hundred and fifty-four stanzas, comprising forty-four thousand six hundred and sixty-eight lines, would have wearied out the industry of any mind whose powers were not indefatigable. He died, too, before his magnificent design was complete, or the elaborate monument of his fame might have been still more colossal. Superiority to mental indolence, so manifest in the lives of Shakspeare and Spenser, is equally noticeable in the cases of Chaucer and Milton, of Ben Jonson and Beaumont and Fletcher, of Dryden and Pope, of Byron and Wordsworth, our other great poets; and, indeed, in the histories of the great poets of all nations. When the quantity of their composition is considered, and it is remembered how much thought must have been expended in the bringing together of choice materials, how much care in the polishing and adorning of each part, and of the whole, of their seemly fabrics, the degree of perseverance exercised in the erection of so many immortal superstructures of the mind is presented to reflection with commanding self-evidence. But let us track, more circumstantially, the life-path, so proverbial for vicissitude, of some of the children of genius, that we may see how the energy of true men is neither quelled by difficulty nor enervated by success.

JOHNSON,

Afterwards so famous as the great arbiter of literary criticism, is found leaving college without a degree, and, from sheer poverty, at the age of twenty-two. The sale of his deceased father's effects, a few months after, affords him but twenty pounds, and he is constrained to become an usher in a grammar school in Leicestershire. In the next year he performs a translation of "Lobo's Voyage to Abyssinia" for a Birmingham bookseller, returns to Lichfield, his birth-place, and publishes proposals for printing, by subscription, the Latin poems of Politian, the life of that author, and a history of Latin poetry from the era of Petrarch to the time of Politian. His project failed to attract patrons, and he next offered his services to Cave, the original projector of the "Gentleman's Magazine." Cave accepted his offer, but on conditions which compelled Johnson to make application elsewhere for earning the means of living. He again offered to become assistant to the master of a grammar school; but, in spite of the great learning he had even then acquired, he was rejected, from the fear that his peculiar nervous and involuntary gestures would render him an object of ridicule with his pupils. Such was one of the disabilities of constitution under which this humbly-born and strong-minded man laboured through life.

Won, not by his ungainly person, but by the high qualities of his mind, a widow, with a little fortune of eight hundred pounds, yielded him her hand, in this season of his poverty; and he immediately opened a classical school in his native town. The celebrated Garrick, then about eighteen years old, became his pupil. His scheme, however, did not succeed; his newly acquired property was exhausted; and he and Garrick, then eight years his junior, set out together for London, with the resolve to seek their fortunes in the larger world. Garrick in a short time was acknowledged as the first genius on the stage, and made his way to wealth almost without difficulty. A longer and more toilful period of trial fell to the lot of the scholar and author. He first offered to the booksellers a manuscript tragedy, supposed to be his "Irene," but could find no one willing to accept it. Cave gave him an engagement to translate the "History of the Council of Trent." He received forty-nine pounds for part of the translation, but it was never completed for lack of sale. His pecuniary condition was so low, soon after this, that he and Savage, having walked, conversing, round Grosvenor Square, till four in the morning, and beginning to feel the want of refreshment, could not muster between them more than fourpence-halfpenny! He received ten guineas for his celebrated poem of "London;" but though Pope said, "The author, whoever he was, could not be long concealed," no further advantage was derived by Johnson from its publication. Hearing of a vacancy in the mastership of another grammar school in Leicestershire, he, once more, proceeds thither as a candidate. The consequences of the poverty which had prevented him from remaining at the university till he could take a degree were now grievously felt. The statutes of the place required that the person chosen should be a Master of Arts. Some interest was made to obtain him that degree from the Dublin University; but it failed, and he was again thrown back on London.

In spite of his melancholic constitution, these repeated disappointments, so far from filling him with despair, seem only to have quickened his invention, and strengthened his resolution to continue the struggle for fame. He formed numerous projects on his return to the metropolis; but none succeeded except his contributions to the "Gentleman's Magazine;" these were, chiefly, the "Parliamentary Debates," which the world read with the belief that they were thus becoming acquainted with the eloquence of Chatham, Walpole, and their compeers, and little dreaming that those speeches were "written in a garret in Exeter Street," by a poverty-stricken author. The talent displayed in this anonymous labour did not serve, as yet, to free him from difficulties. He next undertook to collect and arrange the tracts forming the miscellany, entitled "Harleian." Osborne, the bookseller, was his employer in this work; and, having purchased Lord Oxford's library, the bookseller also employed Johnson to form a catalogue. To relieve his drudgery, Johnson occasionally paused to peruse the book that came to hand; Osborne complained of this; a dispute arose; and the bookseller, with great roughness, gave the author the lie. The incident so characteristic of Johnson, and so often related, now took place—Johnson seized a folio, and knocked the bookseller down. The act was far from justifiable; but his indignation under the offence must have been great, as his rigid adherence to speaking the truth was so observable, that one of his most intimate friends declared "he always talked as if he were speaking on oath."

He escaped, at length, from some degree of the humiliation which attaches to poverty. He projected his great work—the English Dictionary; several of the wealthiest booksellers entered into the scheme, and Johnson now left lodging in the courts and alleys about the Strand, and took a house in Gough Square, Fleet Street. This did not occur till he was eight-and-thirty; so great a portion of life had he passed in almost perpetual contest with pecuniary difficulties; nor was he entirely freed from them for some years to come. During the years spent in the exhausting labour of his Dictionary, the fifteen hundred guineas he received for the copyright were consumed on amanuenses, and the provision necessary for himself and his wife. The

"Rambler" was written during these years in which his Dictionary was in course of publication, and the circumstances of its composition are most note-worthy among the "Triumphs of Perseverance." With the exception of five numbers, every essay was written by Johnson himself; and it was regularly issued every Tuesday and Friday, for two years. The perseverance which enabled him so punctually to execute a stated task, even while continuously labouring in the greater work in which he was engaged, is remarkable: but the young reader's thought ought to be more deeply fixed on the consideration that a life of unremitting devotion to study— unconquered by difficulty, and straitness of circumstances—had rendered him able easily to pour forth the treasures of a full mind. Although apparently the product of great care, and stored with the richest moral reflections, these essays were usually written in haste, frequently while the printer's boy was waiting, and not even read over before given to him. This was not recklessness in Johnson, though it would have been folly in one whose mind was not most opulently stored with matured thought, and who had not attained such a habit of modulating sentences, as to render it almost mechanical. Such attainments can only be reached by the most determined disciple of perseverance. "A man may write at any time, if he will set himself doggedly to it," was Johnson's own saying; but he could not have verified it, unless his mind, by assiduous application, had been filled with the materials of writing. He was, likewise, held in high celebrity as the best converser of his age; but he acknowledged that he had attained his extraordinary accuracy and flow of language by having early laid it down as a fixed rule to arrange his thoughts before expressing them, and never to suffer a careless or unmeaning expression to escape from him.

The profits of a second periodical, "The Idler," and the subscriptions for his edition of Shakspeare, were the means by which he supported himself for the four or five years immediately preceding the age of fifty. His wife had already died, and his aged mother being near her dissolution, in order to reach Lichfield, and pay her the last offices of filial piety, he devoted one fortnight to the composition of his beautiful and immortal tale of "Rasselas," for which he received one hundred pounds. He did not arrive in time to close her eyes, but saw her decently interred, and then hastened back to London, to go, once more, into lodgings and retrench expenses. The next three years of his life appear to have been passed in even more than his early poverty; but the end of his difficulties was approaching.

The last twenty-two years of his existence—from the age of fifty-three to seventy-five—were spent in the receipt of a royal pension of three hundred pounds per annum; in the society of persons of fortune, who considered themselves honoured by the company of the once poverty-stricken and unknown scholar; in the companionship of Edmund Burke, and Oliver

Goldsmith, and Sir Joshua Reynolds, and Joseph Warton, and others whose names are durably written on the roll of genius, and in the receipt of the highest honours of learning—for the Universities, both of Dublin and Oxford, conferred upon him the degree of Doctor of Laws, and the Oxford University had previously sent him the degree of Master of Arts. Regarded as the great umpire of literary taste, receiving deference and respect wherever he went, and no longer driven to his pen by necessity, this honoured exemplar of perseverance did not pass through his remaining course in unproductive indolence. In addition to less important works, his "Lives of the Poets" was produced in this closing period of his life, and is well known as the most valuable and useful of his labours, with the exception of his great Dictionary.

WILLIAM GIFFORD,

In the early circumstances of his life, is a still more striking exemplar of the virtue of perseverance. He was left an orphan at thirteen years of age, was sent to sea for a twelvemonth, and was then taken home by his godfather, who had seized upon whatever his mother had left, as a means of repaying himself for money lent to her, and was now constrained to pay some attention to the boy, by the keen remonstrances of his neighbours. He was sent to school, and made such rapid progress in arithmetic that, in a few months, he was at the head of the school, and frequently assisted his master. The receipt of a trifle for these services raised in him the thought of one day becoming a schoolmaster, in the room of a teacher in the town of Ashburton, who was growing old and infirm. He mentioned his scheme to his godfather, who treated it with contempt, and forthwith apprenticed him to a shoemaker. His new master subjected him to the greatest degradation, made him the common drudge of his household, and took from him the means of pursuing his favourite study of arithmetic.

"I could not guess the motives for this at first," he says—for his narrative is too remarkable at this period of his struggles, to be told in any other than his own language—"but at length discovered that my master destined his youngest son for the situation to which I aspired. I possessed, at this time, but one book in the world, it was a treatise on algebra, given to me by a young woman, who had found it in a lodging-house. I considered it as a treasure, but it was a treasure locked up, for it supposed the reader to be well acquainted with simple equations, and I knew nothing of the matter. My master's son had purchased 'Fenning's Introduction;' this was precisely what I wanted; but he carefully concealed it from me, and I was indebted to chance alone for stumbling upon his hiding-place. I sat up for the greatest part of several nights, successively; and, before he suspected that his treatise was discovered, had completely mastered it. I could now enter upon my own, and that carried me pretty far into the science. This was not done without difficulty. I had not a farthing on earth, nor a friend to give me one; pen, ink, and paper, therefore, were, for the most part, as completely out of my reach as a crown and sceptre. There was, indeed, a resource, but the utmost caution and secrecy were necessary in applying to it. I beat out pieces of leather as smooth as possible, and wrought my problems on them with a blunted awl; for the rest, my memory was tenacious, and I could multiply and divide by it to a great extent."

He essayed the composition of rhyme, and the rehearsal of his verses secured him a few pence from his acquaintances. He now furnished himself with pens, ink, and paper, and even bought some books of geometry and of the higher branches of algebra; but was obliged to conceal them, and to pursue his studies by continued caution. Some of his verses, however, were shown to his master, and were understood to contain satirical reflections upon his oppressor. His books and papers were seized upon, by way of punishment; and he was reduced to the deepest despair. "I look back," he says, in his own admirable narrative, "on that part of my life which immediately followed this event with little satisfaction: it was a period of gloom, and savage unsociability: by degrees I sunk into a kind of corporeal torpor; or, if roused into activity by the spirit of youth, wasted the exertion in splenetic and vexatious tricks, which alienated the few acquaintances compassion had left me."

The heart revolts at the brutal injustice which drove Gifford's young nature thus to harden itself into gloomy endurance of his lot, by "savage unsociability;" but a mind like his could not take that stamp for life. His disposition grew again buoyant, and his aspirations began to rekindle, as the term of his bondage grew shorter. Had he found no deliverance till it had legally expired, it may be safely affirmed that he would then have forced his way into eminence by self-assisted efforts; but an accidental circumstance emancipated him a year before the legal expiry of his apprenticeship. Mr. Cookesley, a philanthropic surgeon, having learnt from Gifford himself the facts of his hard history, through mere curiosity awakened by hearing some of his rhymes repeated, started 'A subscription for purchasing the remainder of the time of William Gifford, and for enabling him to improve himself in writing and English grammar.' Enough was collected to satisfy his master's demand, he was placed at school with a clergyman, made his way into the classics, displayed such diligence that more money was raised to continue him in his promising course; and in two years and two months from the day of his liberation, he was considered by his instructor to be fit for the University, and was sent to Exeter College, Oxford.

Perseverance! what can it not effect? It enabled Gifford to surmount difficulties arising from the most vulgar and brutifying influences, and to make his way triumphantly into an intellectual region of delectable enjoyment. From a boy neglected and degraded—from a youth baffled and thwarted in his aims at a higher state of existence than that of merely living to labour in order to eat, drink, and be clothed—from one fastening his desire upon knowledge, only to be scorned and mocked, and treated as a criminal where he was meriting applause—from a poor pitiable straggler longing for mental breathing-room, amid the coarse conversation he would undoubtedly hear from his master, and those who were his associates, and sinking for some period into sullen despair with his hardship, that like an untoward sky seemed to promise no break of relieving light—he becomes a glad and easier student; is enabled not merely 'to improve himself in writing and English grammar,' but, in six-and-twenty months, becomes a converser, in their own noble language, with the great spirits of Rome and Greece: and enters the most venerable arena of learning in Britain, to become a rival in elegant scholarship with the young heirs to coronets and titles, and to England's widest wealth and influence. What a change did those ancient halls of architectural grandeur, with all their associations of great intellectual names, present for the young and ardent toiler who, but six-and-twenty months before, had bent over the *last* from morning to night, shut out from all that could cheer or elevate the mind, and surrounded with nought but that which tended to disgust and degrade it!

Nor did the career of the young disciple of perseverance, when arrived at his new and loftier stage of struggle, discredit the foresight of those who had assisted him. His first benefactor died before Gifford took his degree, but he was enabled by the generosity of Lord Grosvenor to pursue his studies at the University to a successful issue. After some absence on the continent, as travelling tutor to the nobleman just mentioned, he entered on his course as an author, and gained some distinction; but won his chief celebrity, as well as most substantial rewards, while Editor of the "Quarterly Review"—an office he held from the commencement of that periodical, 1809, till his death, on the last day of 1826, when he had reached the age of seventy-one. In the performance of this critical service he had a salary of one thousand a year; and it is a noble conclusion to the history of this successful scholar of Perseverance, that true-hearted gratitude led him to bequeath the bulk of his fortune to Mr. Cookesley, the son of his early benefactor.

The superiority of genius to difficulties, and the certainty with which it achieves high triumphs through longer or shorter paths of vicissitude, might be shown from the memoirs of Erasmus, and Mendelsohn, and Goldsmith, and Holcroft, and Kirke White, and others, almost a countless host. Early poverty may be said, however, to stimulate the children of Genius to exertion; and its influence may be judged to weaken the merit of their perseverance, since their triumphs may be dated from deep desire to escape from its disadvantages. That such a feeling has been participated by many, or all, of the illustrious climbers after literary distinction, it may not be denied; though the world usually attributes more to its workings in the minds of men of genius than the interior truth, if known, would warrant: the strong necessity to create—the restless power to embody their thinkings—these deep-seated springs of exertion in intellectual men, if understood, would afford a truer solution of their motives for beginning, and the determination to excel for continuing their course, than any mere sordid impulses with which they are often charged. Let us turn to a celebrated name, around which no irksome influences of poverty gathered, either at the outset of his life, or in his progress to literary distinction. His systematic direction of the knowledge acquired by inquiries as profound as they were diversified, and his application of the experience of life, alike to the same great end, afford an admirable spectacle of the noblest perseverance, and of memorable victory over the seductions of ease and competence.

GIBBON,

The author of the unrivalled "Decline and Fall of the Roman Empire," was born to considerable fortune. He left the University at eighteen, after great loss of time, as he tells us in his instructive autobiography, and with what was worse, habits of expense and dissipation. His father being under distressing anxiety on account of his son's irregularities, and, afterwards, from what he deemed of greater moment, young Gibbon's sudden avowal of conversion to the doctrines of the Roman Catholic church, placed him abroad, under the strict care of a Protestant minister. Gibbon began to awake to reflection; and, without prescription from his new guardian, voluntarily entered on severe study. He diligently translated the best Roman writers, turned them into French, and then again into Latin, comparing Cicero and Livy, and Seneca and Horace, with the best orators and historians, philosophers and poets, of the moderns. He next advanced to the Greek, and pursued a similar course with the treasures of that noble literature. He afterwards commenced an inquiry into the Law of Nations, and sedulously perused the treatises of Grotius, Puffendorf, Locke, Bayle, and Montesquieu, the acknowledged authorities on that great subject. He mentions three books which absorbed more than the usual interest he felt in whatever he read: "Pascal's Provincial Letters," the "Abbe de la Bléterie's Life of the Emperor Julian," and "Giannone's Civil History of Naples:" the character of these works shadows forth the grand design which was gradually forming in his mind.

Yet without method, without taking care to store up this various knowledge in such a mode that it might not be mere lumber in the memory, he speedily discerned that even years spent in industrious reading would be, comparatively, of little worth. He, therefore, began to digest his various reading in a common-place book, according to the method recommended by Locke. The eager and enthusiastic student—for such he had now become— by this systematic arrangement of his knowledge under heads, perceived his wants more distinctly, and entered into correspondence for the solution of historic difficulties, with some of the most illustrious scholars of his time, among whom were Professors Crevier of Paris, Breittinger of Zurich, and Matth. Gesner of Göttingen. From each of these learned men he received such flattering notice of the acuteness of his inquiries, as proved how well he had employed the time and means at his command. His first work, written in French, the "Essay on the Study of Literature," was produced at three-and-twenty, after his laborious reading of the best English and French, as well as Latin and Greek authors.

A transition was now made by him, from retired leisure to active life. His father was made major of the Hampshire Militia, himself captain of grenadiers, and the regiment was called out on duty. He had to devote two years and a half to this employ, and expresses considerable discontent with his "wandering life of military servitude;" but thus judiciously tempers his observations: "In every state there exists, however, a balance of good and evil. The habits of a sedentary life were usefully broken by the duties of an active profession."... "After my foreign education, with my reserved temper, I should long have continued a stranger to my native country, had I not been shaken in this various scene of new faces and new friends; had not experience forced me to feel the characters of our leading men, the state of parties, the forms of office, and the operation of our civil and military system. In this peaceful service I imbibed the rudiments and the language and science of tactics, which opened a new field of study and observation.... The discipline and evolutions of a modern battalion gave me a clearer notion of the phalanx and the legion; and the captain of the Hampshire grenadiers has not been useless to the historian of the Roman empire."

Let the young reader observe how, even when a purpose is not as yet distinctly formed, the leading events of life, as well as study, may be made by the regal mind to bend and contribute to the realising of one. Our great paramount duty is to husband time well, to let not an hour glide uselessly, to go on extending our range of knowledge, and resolving to act our part well, even while we are in uncertainty as to what our part may be. The seed well sown, the germs well watered, and a useful harvest must result, though neither we, nor any who look on, for a while, may be able to prophesy of the quality or abundance of the grain, seeing it is but yet in its growth. "From my early youth I aspired to the character of an historian," says Gibbon; "while I served in the militia, before and after the publication of my 'Essay,' this idea ripened in my mind."

Yet, he was for a time undecided as to a subject: the Expedition of Charles the Eighth of France into Italy; the Crusade of Cœur de Lion; the Barons' Wars against John and Henry the Third; the History of Edward the Black Prince; Lives and comparisons of Henry the Fifth and the Emperor Titus; the Life of Sir Philip Sidney, of the Marquis of Montrose, of Raleigh—and other subjects of high interest, but each and all inferior to the one he at length undertook, and for which his studies had all along peculiarly fitted him, successively attracted his attention. Amidst the colossal ruins of the amphitheatre of Titus, the idea at length was formed in his mind of tracing the vicissitudes of Rome; and this idea swelled until his conception extended to such a history as should depicture the thousand years of change which fill up the period between the reign of the Antonines and the conquest of Constantinople by the Turks. Years of laborious study and research were necessary to accomplish this gigantic labour; but it was perfected, and remains the grandest historic monument ever raised by an Englishman. The recent investigations of Guizot have more fully confirmed the fact of the minute and careful inquiries of Gibbon, in bringing together the vast and multifarious materials necessary for the accurate completion of his design. His great work is, emphatically, for strictness of statement, combined with such comprehensiveness of subjects, for depth and clearness of disquisition, and for splendour of style, one of the most magnificent "Triumphs of Perseverance."

And is the roll of these triumphs complete? Have the labours of the past pretermitted the possibility of equal victories in the future? Never, while the human mind exists, can the catalogue of its successes be deemed to have found a limit or an end. Immense fields of history remain yet untrodden and uncultivated; innumerable facts throughout the ages which are gone remain to be collected by industry and arranged by judgment; the ever-varying phases of human affairs offer perpetual material for new chronicle: let none who meditates to devote his youth to historical inquiry, with the meritorious resolve to distinguish his manhood by some useful monument of solid thought, imagine that his ground has been narrowed, but rather understand that it has been cleared and enlarged by the noble workmen who have gone before.

Neither let the young and gifted, in whom the kindlings of creative genius are felt, listen to the dull voices who say, "The last epic has been written—no more great dramas shall be produced—the lyrics of the past will never be equalled!" If such vaticinations were true, it would show that the human mind was dwarfed. Shakspere did not believe that, or he would not have excelled Sophocles. None but intellectual cravens will affright themselves with the belief that they cannot equal the doings of those who have gone before. True courage says, "The laurel is never sere: its leaves are evergreen. The laurels have not all been won: they flourish still, in abundance. The bright examples of the past shall not deter, but cheer me. I will go on to equal them. My life, like the lives of the earth's truly great, shall be devoted to thought, to research—to deep converse with the mighty spirits who still live in their works, though their clay is dissolved; I will prepare to build, and build carefully and wisely, as they built; I also will rear my lasting memorial among "The Triumphs of Perseverance!"

CHAPTER III.
ARTISTS.

CANOVA.—CHANTREY.—SALVATOR ROSA.—BENJAMIN WEST.

If a rude image of the South Sea islanders be compared with one of Chantrey's sculptures, or a Chinese picture with some perfect performance of Raffaelle or Claude, what a world of reflection unfolds itself on the countless steps taken by the mind, from its first attempt at imitating the human form, or depicturing a landscape, to the periods of its most successful effort in statuary or painting. The first childish essay of a great artist, compared with one of the masterpieces of his maturity, calls up kindred thoughts. How often must the eye re-measure an object; how often retrace the direction or inclination of the lines by which a figure is bounded; what an infinite number of comparisons must perception store up in the memory, as to the resemblance of one form to another; what repeated scrutiny must the judgment exercise over what most delights the ideal faculty, till the source of delight—the harmony arising from combination of forms—be discovered and understood; and how unweariedly must the intellect return, again and again, to these its probationary labours, before the capability for realising great triumphs in Art be attained.

Doubtless, the mind of a young artist, like the mind under any other process of training, exercises many of these acts with little self-consciousness; but observation and comparison have, inevitably, to be practised, and their results to be stored up in the mind, before the hand can be directed and employed in accurate delineation and embodiment of forms. Without diligence in this training, the chisel of Chantrey would have failed to bring more life-like shapes from a block of marble than the knife of a Sandwich islander carves out of the trunk of a tree; and the canvas of Claude would have failed as utterly to realise proportion, and sunlight, and distance, as a piece of porcelain figured and coloured by a native of China. As it is in the elaboration of Literature's most perfect products so it is in Art: into the mind his images must be taken; there they must be wrought up into new combinations and shapes of beauty or of power; and from this grand repository the statuary or painter, like the poet, must summon his forms anew, evermore returning, dutifully, to compare them with Nature and actual life, and sparing no effort to clothe them with the attribute of veri-similitude.

Need it be argued, then, that without *perseverance* the world would have beheld none of the wonders of high Art? If the mind, by her own mysterious power, have, first, to pencil the forms of the outward upon her tablets within; if she have, then, a greater work of combination and creation to perform, ere a statue or a picture of the ideal can be realised; if the hand, in a word, can only successfully carve, limn, and colour, from the pattern laid up in the wealth of the trained and experienced mind, how absolute the necessity for perseverance to enrich and perfect that mind which is to direct the hand! That neglect of this evident truth has marked the lives of unsuccessful artists may, too often, be seen in the records of them: while the deepest conviction of a duty to obey its dictates has distinguished the world's most glorious names in painting and sculpture. Let us glance at the steps taken by a few of these, in their way to *triumphs*; not unheedful, meanwhile, how their exhibition of the great moral quality of perseverance enabled them to trample on the difficulties of actual life, as well as to overcome obstacles in their progress to perfect art.

ANTONIA CANOVA,

The greatest of modern sculptors, was born in a mud-walled cabin of an Alpine valley within the Venetian territories; and remained in the care of Pasino, his grandfather, who was a stone-cutter, till his twelfth year. Pasino, evermore employing enticement and tenderness rather than compulsion began to instruct the child in drawing, as soon as his little hand could hold a pencil; and even taught him to model in clay at an early age. At nine years old, however, he was set to work at stone-cutting; and, thenceforward, his essays in art were but pursued as relaxations. Yet his boyish performances were sufficiently remarkable to attract notice from the chief of the patrician family of Falieri, for whom Pasino worked. This nobleman took young Canova under his patronage, and placed him with Toretto, a sculptor. His new preceptor was not very liberal in his instructions; but the young genius secretly pursued his high bent, and one day surprised Toretto by producing the figures of two angels of singular beauty. His yearnings after excellence, at this period, grew vast; but were indefinite. He often became disgusted with what he had done; and to fitful dreams of beauty in Art succeeded moods of despair; but he invariably returned to his models, imperfect as he perceived them to be, and resolved to labour on from the point of his present knowledge up to the mastery he coveted.

On the death of Toretto, in Canova's fifteenth year, Falieri removed the aspiring boy to Venice. He was lodged in his patron's palace; but was too truly a man, in spite of his youth, to brook entire dependence on another, and formed an engagement to work during the afternoons for a sculptor in the city. "I laboured for a mere pittance, but it was sufficient," is the language of one of his letters. "It was the fruit of my own resolution; and, as I then flattered myself, the foretaste of more honourable rewards—for I never thought of wealth." Under successive masters, Canova acquired a knowledge of what were then held to be the established rules of sculpture, but made no important essay, except his Eurydice, which was of the size of nature, and had "great merit" in the estimation of his patron, although Canova himself thought not so highly of it. Indeed, his genius was preparing to break away from the mannerism of his instructors almost as soon as it was learnt. The works of Bernini, Algardi, and other comparatively inferior artists, were then taken for models rather than the Apollo, the Laocoon, the Venus, or the Gladiator—the transcendent remains of ancient statuary. "The unaffected majesty of the antique," observes Mr. Mernes, Canova's English biographer, was then "regarded as destitute of force and impression." And as for Nature, "her simplicity was then considered as poverty, devoid of elegance or grace." Nature, therefore, was not imitated by this school of sculptors; but, in the critical language of one of their own countrymen, she was but "translated according to conventional modes." Canova spurned subjection to the trammels of corrupt taste; and, after deep thought, his resolve was taken, and he entered on a new and arduous path. He thenceforth "took Nature as the text, and formed the commentary from his own elevated taste, fancy, and judgment."

The exhibition of his Orpheus, the companion-statue to his Eurydice, in his twentieth year, gave commencement to Canova's success and reputation, and proved the devotion with which he had applied himself to the study of the anatomy of life, to whatever he observed to be striking in the attitudes of living men, in the expression of their countenances, in "the sculpture of the heart." (*Il scolpir del cuore*), as he so beautifully termed it. His style was foreign to prevailing false taste; but it was so true to Nature that its excellence won him general admiration.

Rome, the great capital of Art, naturally became the theatre of his ambition at this period; and, soon after his twenty-third birthday, he enters on his career in the Eternal City, under the patronage of the Venetian ambassador, obtained through Falieri's friendship. With rapture he beheld a mass of marble, which had cost what would equal sixty-three pounds sterling, arrive at the ambassador's palace, as an assurance that he would have the material for accomplishing a great work he had devised. Yet, with an overawed sense of the perfection he now saw in the remains of ancient sculpture, and believing himself deficient in the conception of ideal beauty, he studied deeply and worked in secret, shutting himself up in a room of the ambassador's palace, after each daily visit to the grand galleries. His Theseus and Minotaur was, at length, shown; and he was considered to have placed himself at the head of living sculptors.

Ten successive years of his life, after this triumph, were devoted to funeral monuments of the Popes Clement the Fourteenth (Ganganelli), and Clement the Twelfth (Rezzonico). "They were," says his biographer, "years of unceasing toil and solicitude, both as the affairs of the artist did not permit of having recourse to the assistance of inferior workmen, and as he meditated technical improvements and modes of execution unknown to contemporaries. Much valuable time was thus lost to all the nobler purposes of study, while the conducting from their rude and shapeless state to their final and exquisite forms such colossal masses was no less exhausting to the mind than to the body. The method, however, which was now first adopted, and subsequently perfected, not only allowed, in future, exclusive attention to the higher provinces of art, but enabled this master to produce a greater number of original works than any other of modern times can boast." These observations show Canova to have been one of the noblest disciples of perseverance; slighting the readier triumphs he might have won, by exerting his skill with the customary appliances, he aimed to invent methods whereby gigantic works in art might be more readily achieved, both by himself and his successors: he prescribed for himself the work of a discoverer, and he magnanimously toiled till he succeeded.

Canova's most perfect works were, of course, accomplished in his full manhood. These were his Cupid and Psyche, Venus, Perseus, Napoleon,

Boxers, and Hercules and Lichas: creations which have made so truthfully applicable to his glorious genius the immortal line of Byron:

"Europe, the world, has but one Canova."

Titles of honour were showered on him during his latter years; among the rest that of "Marquis of Ischia;" but he esteemed all of them as inferior to the triumph of his advocacy for the restoration of the precious works of ancient art to Italy. He was commissioned by the Pope for this undertaking, and his great name will be imperishably united with the memory of its success.

To all who are commencing the struggle of life the moral course of Canova demands equally close imitation, with his persevering zeal in the attainment of artistic excellence. He ever refused pecuniary dependence; subjected himself to great disadvantages in carrying out his designs, rather than submit to such dependence; and when a pension of three thousand crowns was conferred upon him, towards the close of his career, he refused to apply any portion of it to his own gratification of a personal kind, and systematically devoted it, yearly, to premiums for young competitors in art, instruction of scholars in painting and sculpture, and pensions for poor and decayed artists. Young reader, let the words of Canova, on his death-bed, sink deeply into your mind, that they may actuate your whole life as fully and nobly as they actuated his own:—"First of all we ought to do our own duty; but—*first of all!*"

CHANTREY,

The most eminent of our sculptors, was another noble example of successful perseverance. From a boy, accustomed to drive an ass laden with sand into Sheffield, he rose to the highest honours of an exalted profession; a large proportion of the persons of rank and distinction in his own time sat to him for busts and statues: he was knighted, and, like Canova, left considerable wealth at his death, to be devoted through future time to the encouragement of Art. His father, who was a small farmer in the neighbourhood of Sheffield, wished to place him with a grocer or an attorney; but, at his own urgent desire, he was apprenticed with a carver and gilder in that town. An engraver and portrait-painter, perceiving his devotion to Art, gave him some valuable instruction; but his master did not incline to forward his favourite pursuits, fearing they would interfere with his duties as an apprentice. Young Chantrey, however, resolved not to be defeated in his aims, and hired a room for a few pence a week, secretly making it his studio. His apprenticeship to the carver and gilder having expired, he advertised in Sheffield to take portraits in crayons; and two years afterwards announced that he had commenced taking models from the life. Like Canova, but untaught, he began to model in clay when a child; and, at two-and-twenty, he thus began to realise his early bent. Yet patronage was but scanty at Sheffield, and he successively visited Dublin, Edinburgh, and London, working as a modeller in clay. But neither in these larger arenas of merit did he immediately succeed according to his wish. Returning to Sheffield, he modelled four busts of well-known characters there as large as life, one of them being the likeness of the lately-deceased vicar. This was a performance of such excellence that he was offered a commission, by a number of the deceased clergyman's friends, to execute a monument to the same reverend personage for the parish church. Chantrey had never yet lifted chisel to marble; and it, therefore, required all the courage which consciousness of genius alone could give to undertake such a task. It was the great turning point of his life. He accepted the commission, employed a marble mason to rough-hew the block, set about the completion himself, and finished it most successfully. Thenceforward his course was open to the excellence he displayed in giving life-like expression to historic portraits, as in his marble statue of Watt in Westminster Abbey, and his bronze statue of Pitt in Hanover Square; and, above all, in infusing poetry into marble, as in his exquisite sculpture of the Lady Louisa Russell at Woburn Abbey, and his unsurpassed group, "the Sleeping Children," in Lichfield cathedral.

In the lives of the great Michael Angelo himself, of Benvenuto Cellini, and others, may also be found inspiring records of the tameless and tireless energy which has secured to us many of the great triumphs of sculpture. Our limits demand that we devote the remainder of a brief chapter to a glance at the struggles of painters.

SALVATOR ROSA,

One of those high names which are everlasting monuments of the success with which true genius bids defiance to the hostilities of poverty and envy might be claimed, with pride and fondness, by either of the sister arts of Poetry and Music, were it not that his greatest triumphs were won in Painting. The wildness and sublimity of his canvas had their types in the scenery of his birth-place—the ancient and decayed villa of Renella, within view of Mount Vesuvius, and near to Naples. His father was a poverty-stricken artist, and descended from a family to whom poverty and painting had been heirlooms for generations. Determined to avert the continuance of this inauspicious union of inheritances in the life of his child, he took counsel with his wife, and they resolved to dedicate him to the service of the Church. He was, accordingly, taken to the font in the grand church pertaining to the "Monks of the Certosa," and piously named "Salvatore," as a sign and seal of the religious life to which his parents had vowed to devote him. But the method they took to bind him down to religious lessons was not wise, though their meaning was no doubt good; and the boyish Rosa often became a truant, wandered away for days among the rocks and trees, and frequently slept out in the open air of that beautiful climate. His worship of the sublime scenery with which he thus became familiar was soon evinced in the fidelity of numerous sketches of picturesque he drew upon the walls of one of the rooms in the large old house his father inhabited. Unchecked by the reprehension of his parents, who dreaded nothing more than the event of their child becoming an artist, he one day entered the monastery of the Certosa, with his burnt sticks in his hand—his only instruments of design— and began, secretly and silently, to scrawl his wild sketches upon such vacant spaces as he could find, on walls that abounded in the most splendid decorations of gold and vermilion and ultra-marine. The monks caught him at his daring labour, and inflicted upon him a severe whipping; but neither did this subdue his thirst to become an artist.

The perplexity of Salvator's parents was now very great, and they saw no chance of restraining the wayward spirit of their boy but in confiding him to

other tutelage; not reflecting that he had displayed talents which it was peculiarly in their own power to direct and foster into a perfection, the result of which might have been their own relief and their child's happiness. He was, at length, sent to a monastic school; and "Salvatoriello," the nickname his restlessness and ingenious caprices had gained him, was thenceforth clad in the long gown of a monk, in common with his young schoolfellows. Repulsive as confinement might prove to his vehement disposition, it was at this period that his mind received the solid culture which enabled it to produce claims to literary distinction at a future time. So long as his lessons were confined to Homer, Horace, and Sallust, he manifested no disquiet in his restraint; but when the day came that he must enter on the subtleties of the scholastic philosophy, all his youthful rebelliousness against the forced and injudicious religious tasks imposed on him by his own parents rose up, and he was expelled the school of the monastery for contumacy. The grief of his father and mother, at beholding their boy, in his sixteenth year, thus sent back in disgrace to his indigent home, may be easily conjectured. Yet this heavier disaster does not, in the slightest degree, appear to have opened their eyes, as to the want of judgment they had displayed in their child's training: the mother grew increasingly passionate in her desire that "Salvatoriello" should be a churchman; and the father resolved, let the cast-out schoolboy take whatever stamp he might, he should not, by his parents' help, become a painter.

The occurrence of his eldest sister's marriage to Francanzani, a painter of considerable genius, opened, in another year, the way for Salvator's instruction in the art to which nature so strongly inclined him. He had already essayed his powers in poetry and music, having composed several lyrics, and set them to airs dictated by his own imagination, feeling, and taste. These were great favourites with the crowds of Naples, and were daily sung by the women who sat to knit in the sunshine. His devotion to the composition of canzonets was, however, ardently shared with the novel lessons of the studio, as soon as the house of his sister's husband was opened to him for an asylum from the harshness of his parental home. To the teaching of Francanzani he speedily added the copying of nature in the wilds of his truant childhood: and often, when he returned from the mountains with his primed paper full of sketches, his teacher would pat him on the shoulder encouragingly, and say, "Rub on, rub on, Salvatoriello—that is good!" The great painter often related to his friends, in the after days of his fame, what energy he had derived from those simple words of friendly approbation.

Having learnt the elements of his profession, the young Rosa set out to take his *giro*, according to the custom of all young painters at that period. He did not, however, take his way through the cities of Italy most famous for their galleries of Art, like other youthful artists; but yielding to the bent of his natural genius struck up, adventurously, into the mountains of the Abruzzi and the wilds of Calabria. Here he was taken prisoner by banditti, and suffered great hardships. Whether he escaped from them, or was, in the end, liberated, is not clear; but when he returned to Naples, his mind was full of the wondrous pictures of wild volcanic and forest scenery, and striking forms and features of mountain robbers, which he, forthwith, began to realise.

New and more severe difficulties than he had ever yet had to encounter fell to his lot, at his return. His father died in his arms; a few days after, his brother-in-law, Francanzani, was overwhelmed with poverty, and Salvator was left to struggle for the support of his mother and sisters. Yet his strong spirit did not sink. He laid aside music and poetry, and although too poor to purchase canvas, began to depict his wild conceptions on primed paper; and, at night, used to steal out and sell his sketches to some shrewd Jew chapman for a vile price. His gains were pitiful, but he strove, by redoubled industry, to swell their amount for a sufficient supply of the family's necessities.

An accident served to bring into notice the genius whose high merit had hitherto met with no public recognition. Lanfranco, the artist who, with the courtly Spagnuoletto, shared the patronage of the rich in Naples, stopped his equipage, one day, in the "Street of Charity," and called for a picture to be brought to him which arrested his eye in the collection of one of the *rivendotori*, or second-hand dealers. It was a masterly sketch of "Hagar in the Wilderness," and the obscure name of "Salvatoriello" was subscribed at the corner of it. Lanfranco gave orders that all sketches which could be found bearing that name should be bought for him. Rosa immediately raised his prices; but, although this high acknowledgment of his merit brought him the acquaintance of several influential names in his profession, he was speedily so deeply disgusted with the jealousy and envy of others, that he strapped all his fortune to his back, and at the age of twenty set out on foot to seek better treatment at Rome. There he studied energetically, worshipping, above all, the kindred genius of Michael Angelo; but meeting with a renewal of neglect, and taking a fever from the malaria, once more returned to Naples. The misery in which his family was plunged was still greater than at his departure; and another period of keen life-combat followed. This repeated struggle did not depress him; but it gave his mind that bitter tendency which he afterwards displayed in his poetical "Satires."

At twenty-four, under the humble patronage of a domestic of the Cardinal Brancaccia, he again went to Rome; and through the friendship of the same plain acquaintance had a large and lonely apartment provided for him, as a studio, in the cardinal's palace. Dependence nevertheless revolted his lofty spirit, and he again returned to Naples, but engaged to send his pictures to his friend for public exposure in Rome. His "Prometheus" was the first of his pictures exhibited at one of the annual shows in the Pantheon, and the

public voice adjudged it to be the greatest. He obeyed a renewed invitation to Rome, but it was still to meet with disappointment. The next carnival furnished his versatile genius with an occasion for winning, by humorous stratagem, the attention denied to his more sterling merit. He put on a mask, and played the charlatan and *improvisatore* in the public streets, among a crowd of such exhibitors as abound in Rome at such seasons; but soon eclipsed them all by the splendour of his wit. Curiosity was raised to the highest pitch, at the close of the carnival, respecting the identity of this unequalled exhibitor; and when he was proclaimed to be the painter of the "Prometheus" the admiration was unbounded. Salvator, now, for some successive months, gave himself up to conversaziones, wherever invited; and there, by his wit, his lute, and canzonettes, paved the way for his greater acceptance as a painter.

Jealousy, in that age of corrupt patronage and jealous artists, still pursued him; but his genius, thenceforth, rose above all opposition. His landscapes were in every palace, and he soon rose to affluence. Yet the remainder of his life was chequered with difficulties into which the vehemence of his nature perpetually plunged him. That nature was unsubduable amidst all vicissitudes. The magnificent creations of his "Socrates swallowing Poison," "Purgatory," "Prodigal Son," "St. Jerome," "Babilonia," and "Conspiracy of Catiline," with an almost innumerable catalogue of lesser pieces, flowed from his pencil, during a life alternately marked by devotion to each of the sister Arts, and, during one portion of it, to political contest—for he flew to Naples, with all the ardour of patriotism, and joined Masaniello, in his sincere but short-lived effort to rescue his countrymen from a crushing despotism. His participation in the celebrated fisherman's conspiracy placed him in danger of the Inquisition on his return to Rome; but, on retiring to Florence, he became the favourite of the Grand Duke, Cosmo the Third, and entered on a career of opulent success, which attended him to the end of life.

The life-passages of Salvator Rosa, by injudicious thwarting of his nature, were rendered thorny beyond those of the great majority of men, and the amazing versatility of his talents, combined with almost volcanic ardour of spirit, defied common rules; but the strength of his judgment so completely gave him the victory over influences that might have destroyed him, as to lead him to seek the memorable "Triumphs of Perseverance" he secured by his supreme devotion to that Art, in which there is reckoned no greater name for sublimity and originality, and none of greater general excellence than those of Raffaelle and Michael Angelo. Let the brief sketch of Salvator Rosa be compared with the much more "even tenor" of the life of another, that it may be seen how clearly, in spite of contrast, many of the same valuable lessons are deducible from it.

BENJAMIN WEST,

An American Quaker by birth, was the youngest of a family of ten children, and was nurtured with great tenderness and care; a prophecy uttered by a preacher of the sect having impressed his parents with the belief that their child would, one day, become a great man. In what way the prophecy was to be realised they had formed to themselves no definite idea; but an incident, which occurred in young West's sixth year, led his father to ponder deeply as to whether its fulfilment were not begun. Benjamin, being left to watch the infant child of one of his relatives while it was left asleep in the cradle, had drawn its smiling portrait, in red and black ink, there being paper and pens on the table in the room. This spontaneous and earliest essay of his genius was so strikingly truthful that it was instantly and rapturously recognised by the family. During the next year he drew flowers and birds with pen and ink; but a party of Indians, coming on a visit to the neighbourhood, taught him to prepare and use red and yellow ochre and indigo. Soon after, he heard of camel-hair pencils, and the thought seized him that he could make use of a substitute, so he plucked hairs from the tail of a black cat that was kept in the house, fashioned his new instrument, and began to lay on colours, much to his boyish satisfaction. In the course of another year a visitant friend, having seen his pictures, sent him a box of colours, oils, and pencils, with some pieces of prepared canvas and a few engravings. Benjamin's fascination was now indescribable. The seductions presented by his new means of creation were irresistible, and he played truant from school for some days, stealing up into a garret, and devoting the time, with all the throbbing wildness of delight, to painting. The schoolmaster called, the truant was sought, and found in the garret by his mother. She beheld what he had done; and instead of reprehending him fell on his neck and kissed him, with tears of ecstatic fondness. How different from the training experienced by the poor, persecuted and tormented "Salvatoriello!" What wonder, that the fiery-natured Italian afterwards drew human nature with a severe hand; and how greatly might his vehement disposition have been softened, had his nurture resembled that of the child of these gentle Quakers!

The friend who had presented him with the box of colours some time after took him to Philadelphia, where he was introduced to a painter, saw his pictures, the first he had ever seen except his own, and wept with emotion at the sight of them. Some books on Art increased his attachment to it; and some presents enabled him to purchase materials for further exercises. Up to his eighteenth year, strange as the facts seem, he received no instruction in painting, had to carve out his entire course himself, and yet advanced so far as to create his first historical picture, "The Death of Socrates," and to execute portraits for several persons of taste. His father, however, had never yet assisted him; for, with all his ponderings on the preacher's prophecy, he could not shake off some doubts respecting the lawfulness of the profession of a painter, to which no one of the conscientious sect had ever yet devoted himself. A counsel of "Friends" was therefore called together, and the perplexed father stated his difficulty and besought their advice. After deep consideration, their decision was unanimous that the youth should be permitted to pursue the objects to which he was now both by nature and habit attached; and young Benjamin was called in, and solemnly set apart by the primitive brethren for his chosen profession. The circumstances of this consecration were so remarkable, that, coupled with the early prophecy already mentioned, they made an impression on West's mind that served to strengthen greatly his resolution for advancement in Art, and for devotion to it as his supreme object through life.

On the death of his affectionate mother he finally left his father's house, and, not being yet nineteen, set up in Philadelphia as a portrait-painter, and soon found plenty of employment. For the three or four succeeding years he worked unremittingly, making his second essay at historic painting within that term, but labouring at portraits, chiefly with the view of winning the means to enable himself to visit Italy. His desire was at length accomplished, a merchant of New York generously presenting him with fifty guineas as an additional outfit, and thus assisting him to reach Rome without the uneasiness that would have arisen from straitness of means in a strange land.

The appearance of a Quaker artist of course caused great excitement in the metropolis of Art; crowds of wonderers were formed around him; but, when in the presence of the great relics of Grecian genius, he was the wildest wonderer of all. "How like a young Mohawk!" he exclaimed, on first seeing the "Apollo Belvidere," its life-like perfection bringing before his mind, instantaneously, the free forms of the desert children of Nature in his native America. The excitement of little more than one month in Rome threw him into a dangerous illness, from which it was some time before he recovered. He visited the other great cities of Italy, and also painted and exhibited two great historical pictures, which were successful, ere the three years were completed which he stayed in that country. He would have returned to Philadelphia; but a letter from his father recommended him first to visit England.

West's success in London was speedily so decided, that he gave up all thoughts of returning to America. For thirty years of his life he was chiefly employed in executing, for King George the Third, the great historical and scriptural pictures which now adorn Windsor Palace and the Royal Chapel. After the abrupt termination of the commission given him by the King, he continued still to be a laborious painter. His pictures in oil amount to about four hundred, and many of them are of very large dimensions and contain a great number of figures. Among these may be mentioned, for its wide celebrity, the representation of "Christ healing the Sick," familiar to every visitor of the National Gallery. If polished taste be more highly charmed with other treasures there, the heart irresistibly owns the excellence of this great realisation by the child of the American Quaker. He received three thousand guineas for this picture, and his rewards were of the most substantial kind ever after his settlement in England. He was also appointed President of the Royal Academy, on the death of Sir Joshua Reynolds, and held the office at his own death, in the eighty-second year of his age.

Though exposed to no opposition from envy or jealousy at any time of his career, and though encouraged in his childish bent, and helped by all who knew him and had the power to help him, without Perseverance of the most energetic character Benjamin West would not have continued without pattern or instruction to labour on to excellence, nor would he have sustained his prosperity so firmly, or increased its productiveness so wondrously.

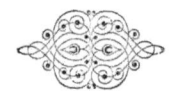

CHAPTER IV.
MUSICIANS.

HANDEL.

The time may come when Music will be universally recognised as the highest branch of Art; as the most powerful divulger of the intellect's profoundest conceptions and noblest aspirations; as the truest interpreter of the heart's loves and hates, joys and woes; as the purest, least sensual, disperser of mortal care and sorrow; as the all-glorious tongue in which refined, good, and happy beings can most perfectly utter their thoughts and emotions. Perhaps this cannot be till the realm of the physical world be more fully subdued by man. The human faculties have hitherto been, necessarily, too much occupied with the struggle for existence, for security against want and protection from the elements, with the invention of better and swifter modes of locomotion and of transmission of thought, to advance to a general apprehension of the superior nature of Music. "Practical men"—men fitted for the discharge of the world's present duties by the manifestation of the readiest and fullest capacity for meeting its present wants—are, naturally and justly, those whom the world most highly values in its current state of civilisation.

This necessary preference of the practical to the ideal may lead many, who cannot spare a thought from the every-day concerns of the world, to deem hastily that the stern and energetic quality of Perseverance cannot be fully developed in the character of a devotee to Music. But, dismissing the greater question just hinted at, it may be replied that it is the evident tendency of man to form the lightest pleasures of the mind, as well as his gravest discoveries, into what is called "science;" and the lives of numerous musicians show that vast powers of application have been continuously devoted to the elaboration of the rules of harmony, while others have employed their genius as ardently in the creation of melody. These creations, when the symbols are learnt in which they are written, the mind, by its refined exorcism, can enable the voice, or the hand of the instrumental performer, to summon into renewed existence to the end of time. Before symbols were invented and rules constructed, the wealth of Music must necessarily have been restricted to a few simple airs such as the memory could retain and easily reproduce. *Perseverance—Perseverance*—has guided and sinewed men's love of the beautiful and powerful in melody and harmony, until, from the simple utterance of a few notes of feeling, rudely conveyed from sire to son by renewed utterance, Music has grown up into a science, dignified and adorned by profound theorists, like Albrechtsberger, and by sublime creative geniuses, such as the majestic Handel and sweetest Haydn and universal Mozart and sublime Beethoven.

For their successful encounter of the great "battle of life," a hasty thinker would also judge that the extreme susceptibility of musicians must unfit them; extreme susceptibility, which is, perhaps, more peculiarly their inheritance than it is that even of poets. Yet the records of the lives of musical men prove, equally with the biographies of artists, authors, and linguists, that true genius, whatever may be the object of its high devotion, is unsubduable by calamity and opposition. The young inquirer will find ample proof of this in various biographies: our limits demand that we confine ourselves to one musician, as an exemplar of the grand attribute of Perseverance.

GEORGE FREDERICK HANDEL,

The first of the four highest names in Music, was the son of a physician of Halle, in Lower Saxony, and was designed by his father for the study of the civil law. The child's early attachment to music—for he could play well on the old instrument called a clavichord before he was seven years old—was, therefore, witnessed by his parent with great displeasure. Unable to resist the dictates of his nature, the boy used to climb up into a lonely garret, shut himself up, and practise, chiefly when the family were asleep. He attached himself so diligently to the practice of his clavichord, that it enabled him, without ever having received the slightest instruction, to become an expert performer on the harpsichord. It was at this early age that the resolution of young Handel was manifested in the singular incident often told of his childhood. His father set out in a chaise to go and visit a relative who was valet-de-chambre to the Duke of Saxe-Weisenfels, but refused to admit the boy as a partner in his journey. After the carriage, however, the boy ran, kept closely behind it for some miles, unconquerable in his determination to proceed, and was at last taken into the chaise by his father. When arrived, it was impossible to keep him from the harpsichords in the duke's palace; and, in the chapel, he contrived to get into the organ-loft, and began to play with such skill on an instrument he had never before touched, that the duke, overhearing him, was surprised, asked who he was, and then used every argument to induce the father to make the child a musician, and promised to patronise him.

Overcome by the reasonings of this influential personage, the physician gave up the thought of thwarting his child's disposition: and, at their return to Halle, placed young Handel under the tuition of Zackau, the organist of the cathedral. The young "giant"—a designation afterwards so significantly bestowed upon him by Pope—grew up so rapidly into mastery of the instrument, that he was soon able to conduct the music of the cathedral in the organist's absence; and, at nine years old, composed church services both for voices and instruments. At fourteen he excelled his master; and his father resolved to send him, for higher instruction, to a musical friend who was a professor at Berlin. The opera then flourished in that city more highly than in any other in Germany; the king marked the precocious genius of the young Saxon, and offered to send him into Italy for still more advantageous study: but his father, who was now seventy years old, would not consent to his leaving his "fatherland."

Handel next went to Hamburgh, where the opera was only little inferior to Berlin. His father died soon after; and, although but in his fourteenth year, the noble boy entered the orchestra as a salaried performer, took scholars, and thus not only secured his own independent maintenance, but sent frequent pecuniary help to his mother. How worshipfully the true children of Genius blend their convictions of moral duty with the untiring aim to excel!

On the resignation of Keser, composer to the opera, and first harpsichord in Hamburgh, a contest for the situation took place between Handel and the person who had hitherto been Keser's second. Handel's decided superiority of skill secured him the office, although he was but fifteen years of age; but his success had nearly cost him his life, for his disappointed antagonist made a thrust with a sword at his breast, where a music book Handel had buttoned under his coat prevented the entrance of the weapon. Numerous sonatas, three operas, and other admired pieces, were composed during Handel's superintendence of the Hamburgh opera; but, at nineteen, being invited by the brother of the Grand Duke, he left that city for Tuscany. He received high patronage at Florence, and afterwards visited Venice, Rome, and Naples, residing, for shorter or longer periods, in each city, producing numerous operas, cantatas, and other pieces, reaping honours and rewards, and becoming acquainted with Corelli, Scarletti, and other musicians; till, after spending six years in Italy, he returned to Germany.

Through the friendship of Baron Kilmansegg he was introduced to the Elector of Hanover, was made "chapel-master" to the court, and had a pension conferred upon him of fifteen hundred crowns a year. In order to secure the services of the "great musician," as he was acknowledged now to be, the King provided that he should be allowed, at will, to be absent for a year at a time. The very next year he took advantage of this provision and set out for England, having first visited his old master Zackau, and his aged and blind mother for the last time—still true, amidst the dazzling influences of his popularity, to the most correct emotions of the heart!

His opera of "Rinaldo" was performed with great success during his stay in this country, and after one year he returned to Hanover; yet his predilection for England, above every other country he had seen, was so strong, that after the lapse of another year he was again in London. The peace of Utrecht occurred a few months after his second arrival, and having composed a Te Deum and Jubilate in celebration of it, and thereby won such favour that Queen Anne was induced to solicit his continuance in England, and to confer upon him a pension of £200 a year, Handel resolved to forfeit his Hanoverian pension, and made up his mind to remain in London. But, two years afterwards, the Queen died, and the great musician was now in deep dread that his slight of the Elector's favours would be resented by that personage on becoming King of England. George the First, indeed, expressed himself very indignantly respecting Handel's conduct; but the Baron Kilmansegg again rendered his friend good service. He instructed Handel to compose music of a striking character, to be played on the water, as the King took amusement with a gay company. Handel created his celebrated "Water Music," chiefly adapted for horns; and the effect was so striking that the King was delighted. Kilmansegg seized the opportunity, and sued for the restoration of his friend to favour. The boon was richly obtained, for Handel's pension was raised to £400 per annum, and he was appointed musical teacher to the young members of the Royal Family.

Prosperity seemed to have selected Handel, up to this period, for her favourite; but severe reverses were coming. The opera in this country had hitherto been conducted on worn-out and absurd principles, and a large body of the people of taste united to promote a reform. Rival opera-houses (as at the present period) were opened; and during nine years Handel superintended one establishment. It was one perpetual quarrel: when his opponents, by any change, had become so feeble that he seemed on the eve of a final triumph, one or other of the singers in his own company would grow unmanageable: Senesino was the chief of these, and Handel's refusal to accept the mediation of several of the nobility, and be reconciled to him, caused the establishment over which he presided to be finally broken up. The great powers of Farinelli, the chief singer at the rival house, to whom an equal could not then be found in Europe, also largely contributed to Handel's ruin. He withdrew, with a loss of ten thousand pounds; his constitution seemed completely broken with the years of harassment he had experienced; and he retired to the baths of Aix-la-Chapelle, scarcely with the hope, on the part of his friends, that they would ever see him in England again.

His paralysis and other ailments, however, disappeared with wondrous suddenness; after he reached the medical waters, he recovered full health and vigour, and, at the age of fifty-two, returned to England with the manly resolve to struggle till he had paid his debts, and once more retrieved a fortune equal to his former condition. It was now that the whole strength of the man was tried. He produced his "Alexander's Feast;" but, in spite of its acknowledged merit, the nobility whom he had offended would not patronise him. He produced other pieces, but they failed from the same cause. He then bent his mighty genius on the creation of newer and grander attractions than had ever been yet introduced in music, and produced his unequalled "Messiah," which was performed at Covent Garden during Lent. Yet the combination against him was maintained, until he sunk into deeper difficulties than ever.

GEORGE FREDERICK HANDEL Esqr
Born February XXIII, MDCLXXXIV.
Died on Good Friday, April XIII, MDCCLIX.

Unsubdued by the failures which had accumulated around him during the five years which had elapsed since his return to England, he set out for Ireland, at fifty-seven, and had his "Messiah" performed in Dublin, for the benefit of the city prison. His success was instantaneous; several performances took place for his own benefit, and the next year he renewed the war against Fortune, in London, by producing his magnificent "Samson," and having it performed, together with his "Messiah," at Covent Garden. The first renewed performance of the "Messiah" was for the benefit of the Foundling Hospital; and the funds of that philanthropic institution were thenceforth annually benefited by the repetition of that sublime Oratorio. Prejudice was now subdued, the "mighty master" triumphed, and his darling wish for honourable independence was fully realised; for more than he had lost was retrieved.

Handel's greatest works, like those of Haydn, were produced in his advanced years. His "Jephthah" was produced at the age of sixty-seven. Paralysis returned upon him at fifty-nine, and *gutta serena*—Milton's memorable affliction—reduced him to "total eclipse" of sight some years after: but he submitted cheerfully to his lot, after brief murmuring, and continued, by dictation to an amanuensis, the creation of new works, and the performance of his Oratorios to the last. He conducted his last Oratorio but a week before his death, and died, as he had always desired to do, on Good Friday, at the age of seventy-five. He was interred, with distinguished honours, among the great and good of that country which had naturalised him, in Westminster Abbey. May the sight of his monument inspire the young reader with an unquenchable zeal to emulate, in whatever path wisdom may direct life to be passed, the moral and intellectual excellencies of this glorious disciple of Perseverance!

CHAPTER V.
SCIENTIFIC DISCOVERERS AND MECHANICIANS.

If great proficiency in tongues, skill to depicture human thought and character, and enthusiastic devotion to art, he worthy of our admiration, the toiling intelligences who have taught us to subdue the physical world, and to bring it to subserve our wants and wishes, claim scarcely less homage. Art and literature could never have sprung into existence if men had remained mere strugglers for life, in their inability to contend with the elements of nature, because ignorant of its laws; and an acquaintance with the languages of tribes merely barbarous would have been but a worthless kind of knowledge. To scientific discoverers—the pioneers of civilization, who make the world worth living in, and render man's tenancy of it more valuable by every successive step of discovery—our primary tribute of admiration and gratitude seems due. They are the grand revealers of the physical security, health, plenty, and means of locomotion, which give the mind vantage-ground for its reach after higher refinement and purer pleasures.

Should the common observation be urged, that many of the most important natural discoveries have resulted from accident, let it be remembered, that, but for the existence of some of our race, more attentive than the rest, Nature might still have spoken in vain, as she had undoubtedly done to thousands before she found an intelligent listener, in each grand instance of physical discovery. Grant all the truth that may attach to the observation just quoted, and yet the weighty reflection remains—that it was only by men who, in the sailor's phrase, were "on the look-out," that the revelations of Nature were caught. The natural laws were in operation for ages, but were undiscovered, because men guessed rather than inquired, or lived on without heed to mark, effort to comprehend, industry to register, and, above all, without perseverance to proceed from step to step in discovery, till entire truths were learnt. That these have been the attributes of those to whom we owe the rich boon of science, a rapid survey of some of their lives will manifest.

SIR HUMPHREY DAVY,

The son of a wood carver of Penzance, was apprenticed by his father to a surgeon and apothecary of that town, and afterwards with another of the same profession, but gave little satisfaction to either of his masters. Natural philosophy had become his absorbing passion; and, even while a boy, he dreamt of future fame as a chemist. The rich diversity of minerals in Cornwall offered the finest field for his empassioned inquiries; and he was in the habit of rambling alone for miles, bent upon his yearning investigation into the wonders of Nature. In his master's garret, and with the assistance of such a laboratory as he could form for himself from the phials and gallipots of the apothecary's shop, and the pots and pans of the kitchen, he brought the mineral and other substances he collected to the test. The surgeon of a French vessel wrecked on the coast gave him a case of instruments, among which was one that he contrived to fashion into an air-pump, and he was soon enabled to extend the range of his experiments; but the proper use of many of the instruments was unknown to him.

JAMES WATT.   SIR HUMPHREY DAVY.

A fortunate accident brought him the acquaintanceship of Davies Gilbert, an eminent man of science. Young Davy was leaning one day on the gate of his father's house, when a friend, who was passing by with Mr. Gilbert, said, "That is young Davy, who is so fond of chemistry." Mr. Gilbert immediately entered into conversation with the youth, and offered him assistance in his studies. By the kind offices of his new friend he was afterwards introduced to Dr. Beddoes, who had formed a pneumatic institution at Bristol, and was in want of a superintendent for it. At the age of nineteen Davy received this appointment, and immediately began the splendid course of chemical discovery which has rendered his name immortal as one of the greatest benefactors as well as geniuses of the race.

At twenty-one he published his "Researches, Chemical and Philosophical, chiefly concerning Nitrous Oxide, and its respiration." The singularly intoxicating quality of this gas when breathed was unknown before Davy's publication of his experiments in this treatise. The attention it drew upon him from the scientific world issued in his being invited to leave Bristol, and take the chair of chemistry which had just been established in the London Royal Institution. Although but a youth of two-and-twenty, his lectures in the metropolis were attended by breathless crowds of men of science and title; and, in another year, he was also appointed Professor of Chemistry to the Board of Agriculture. His lectures in that capacity greatly advanced chemical knowledge, and were published at the request of the Board. When twenty-five he was elected a Fellow of the Royal Society, and, on the death of Sir Joseph Banks, was made its President by a unanimous vote. It was in the delivery of his Bakerian lectures, before this learned body, that he laid the foundation of the new science called "electro-chemistry." The Italians, Volta and Galvani, had some years before discovered and made known the surprising effects produced on the muscles of dead animals by two metals being brought into contact with each other. Davy showed that the metals underwent chemical changes, not by what had been hitherto termed "electricity," but by affinity; and that the same effects might be produced by one of the metals, provided a fluid were brought to act on its surface in a certain manner. The composition and decomposition of substances by the application of the galvanic energy, as displayed in the experiments of the young philosopher, filled the minds of men of science with wonder.

His grand discoveries of the metallic bases of the alkalies and earths, of the various properties of the gases, and of the connexion of electricity and magnetism, continued to absorb the attention of the scientific world through succeeding years; but a simple invention, whereby human life was rescued from danger in mines, the region whence so great a portion of the wealth of England is derived, placed him before the minds of millions, learned and illiterate, as one of the guardians of man's existence. This was the well-known "safety lamp," an instrument which is provided at a trifling expense, and with which the toiling miner can enter subterranean regions unpierceable before, without danger of explosion of the "fire-damp," so destructive, before this discovery, to the lives of thousands. The humblest miner rejects any other name but that of "Davy Lamp" for this apparently insignificant protector; and ventures, with it in his hand, cheerfully and boldly into the realms of darkness, where the "black diamonds" lie so many fathoms beneath the surface of the earth, and, not seldom, under the bed of the sea. The proprietors of the northern coal mines presented the discoverer with a service of plate of the value of £2000, at a public dinner, as a manifestation of their sense of his merits. He was the first person knighted by the Prince Regent, afterwards King George IV., and was a few years after raised to the baronetage. Such honours served to mark the estimation in which he was held by those who had it in their power to confer them; but Davy's enduring distinctions, like those of the unequalled Newton, are derived from the increase of power over nature, which he has secured for millions yet unborn, by the force of his genius, girt up, tirelessly by *Perseverance*, till its grand triumphs were won.

From this hasty survey of the magnificent course of one of the great penetrators into the secrets of nature, and preservers of human life, let us cast a glance on the struggles of one who has been the means of multiplying man's hands and fingers—to use a strong figure—of opening up sources of employment for millions, and of showing the road to wealth for thousands.

SIR RICHARD ARKWRIGHT,

Was a poor barber till the age of thirty, and then changed his trade for that of an itinerant dealer in hair. Nothing is known of any early attachment he had for mechanical inventions; but, about four years after he had given up shaving beards, he is found enthusiastically bent on the project of discovering the "perpetual motion," and, in his quest for a person to make him some wheels, gets acquainted with a clockmaker of Warrington, named Kay. This individual had also been for some time bent on the construction of new mechanic powers, and, either to him alone, or to the joint wit of the two, is to be attributed their entry on an attempt at Preston, in Lancashire, to erect a novel machine for spinning cotton-thread. The partnership was broken, and the endeavour given up, in consequence of the threats uttered by the working spinners, who dreaded that such an invention would rob them of bread, by lessening the necessity for human labour; and Arkwright alone, bent on the accomplishment of the design, went to Nottingham. A firm of bankers in that town made him some advances of capital, with a view to partake in the benefits arising from his invention; but, as Arkwright's first machines did not answer his end efficiently, they grew weary of the connection, and refused further supplies. Unshaken in his own belief of future success, Arkwright now took his models to a firm of stocking weavers, one of whom, Mr. Strutt—a name which has also become eminent in the manufacturing enterprise of the country—was a man of intelligence, and of some degree of acquaintance with science. This firm entered into a partnership with Arkwright, and, he having taken out a patent for his invention, they built a spinning-mill, to be driven by horse-power, and filled it with frames. Two years afterwards they built another mill at Cromford, in Derbyshire, moved by water-power; but it was in the face of losses and discouragements that they thus pushed their speculations. During five years they sunk twelve thousand pounds, and his partners were often on the point of giving up the scheme. But Arkwright's confidence only increased by failure, and, by repeated essays at contrivance, he finally and most triumphantly succeeded. He lived to realise an immense fortune, and his present descendant is understood to be one of the wealthiest persons in the kingdom. The weight of cotton imported now is three hundred times greater than it was a century ago; and its manufacture, since the invention of Arkwright, has become the greatest in England.

Origin of the Stocking-loom.

THE REV. EDMUND CARTWRIGHT, D.D.,

Must be mentioned as the meritorious individual who completed the discovery of cotton manufacture, by the invention of the power-loom. His tendency towards mechanical contrivances had often displayed itself in his youth; but his love of literature, and settlement in the church, led him to lay aside such pursuits as trifles, and it was not till his fortieth year that a conversation occurred which roused his dormant faculty. His own account of it must be given, not only for the sake of its striking character, but for the powerful negative it puts upon the hackneyed observation, that almost all great and useful discoveries have resulted from "accident." The narrative first appeared in the "Supplement to the Encyclopædia Britannica."

"Happening to be at Matlock, in the summer of 1784, I fell in company with some gentlemen of Manchester, when the conversation turned on Arkwright's spinning-machinery. One of the company observed that, as soon as Arkwright's patent expired, so many mills would be erected, and so much cotton spun, that hands would never be found to weave it. To this observation I replied, that Arkwright must then set his wits to work to invent a weaving-mill. This brought on a conversation upon the subject, in which the Manchester gentlemen unanimously agreed that the thing was impracticable, and, in defence of their opinion, they adduced arguments which I was certainly incompetent to answer, or even to comprehend, being totally ignorant of the subject, having never at the time seen a person weave. I controverted, however, the impracticability of the thing by remarking that there had been lately exhibited in London an automaton figure which played at chess. 'Now, you will not assert, gentlemen,' said I, 'that it is more difficult to construct a machine that shall weave, than one that shall make all the variety of moves that are required in that complicated game.' Some time afterwards, a particular circumstance recalling this conversation to my mind, it struck me that, as in plain weaving, according to the conception I then had of the business, there could be only three movements, which were to follow each other in succession, there could be little difficulty in producing and repeating them. Full of these ideas, I immediately employed a carpenter and smith to carry them into effect. As soon as the machine was finished I got a weaver to put in the warp, which was of such materials as sail-cloth is usually made of. To my great delight, a piece of cloth, such as it was, was the produce. As I had never before turned my thoughts to mechanism, either in theory or practice, nor had seen a loom at work, nor knew anything of its construction, you will readily suppose that my first loom must have been a most rude piece of machinery. The warp was laid perpendicularly; the reed fell with a force of at least half-a-hundred weight; and the springs which threw the shuttle were strong enough to have thrown a congreve rocket. In short, it required the strength of two powerful men to work the machine, at a slow rate, and only for a short time. Conceiving, in my simplicity, that I had accomplished all that was required, I then secured what I thought a most valuable property by a patent, 4th of April, 1785. This being done, I then condescended to see how other people wove; and you will guess my astonishment when I compared their easy modes of operation with mine. Availing myself, however, of what I then saw, I made a loom in its general principles nearly as they are now made. But it was not till the year 1787 that I completed my invention, when I took out my last weaving patent, August the 1st of that year."

Challenged by a manufacturer who came to see his machine, to render it capable of weaving checks or fancy patterns, Dr. Cartwright applied his mind to the discovery, and succeeded so perfectly, that when the manufacturer visited him again some weeks after, the visitor declared he was assisted by something beyond human power. Were these discoveries the fruit of "accident," or were they attributable to the power of mind, unswervingly bent to attain its object by Perseverance?

Numerous additional inventions in manufactures and agriculture owe their origin to this good, as well as ingenious man, whose mind was so utterly uncorrupted by any sordid passion that he neglected to turn his discoveries to any great pecuniary benefit, even when secured to him by patent. The merchants and manufacturers of Manchester, however, memorialised the Lords of the Treasury in his behalf, during his latter years, and Parliament made him a grant of 10,000*l.* Dr. Cartwright directed his mind to the steam-engine, among his other thoughts, and told his son, many years before the prophecy was realised, that, if he lived to manhood, he would see both ships and land-carriages moved by steam. From seeing one of his models of a steam-vessel, it is asserted Fulton, then a painter in this country, urged the idea of steam navigation upon his countrymen, on his return to America, until he saw it triumphantly carried out.

The new and vast motive power just mentioned conducts us to another illustrious name in the list of the disciples of Perseverance. Like the names of Newton, Gutenberg the inventor of printing, and a few others, the name to which we allude has claims upon the gratitude of mankind which can never be fully rendered until the entire race participate in the superior civilization it is the certain destiny of these grand discoveries to institute.

JAMES WATT,

Was the son of a small merchant of Greenock, and, on account of his weakly state when a child, was unable at first to enjoy the advantages of school tuition, and was therefore taught chiefly at home. When but six years old he was frequently caught chalking diagrams and solving problems on the hearth; and at fourteen he made a rude electrical machine with his own hands. His aunt, it is related, often chided him for indolence and mischief when he was found playing with the tea-kettle on the fire, watching the steam coming out of the spout, and trying the steam's force by obstructing its escape; the might of the vaporous element seeming even then to have begun to present itself, unavoidably, to his imagination and understanding. He grew to be an extensive manufacturer of philosophical toys while a boy, and used to increase his pocket-money by standing with them at the college gate, in Glasgow, and vending them to the students as they passed out. At eighteen years of age his father apprenticed him to a mathematical instrument maker in London, but in little more than a year his weak health rendered it necessary to send him home to Scotland.

James Watt—when a Boy—playing With the Tea-kettle.

At twenty-one, although he had received so little instruction in that profession, his skill secured him the appointment of mathematical instrument maker to the college of Glasgow. His appointment, however, was not sufficiently productive to render it worth keeping; and, seven years afterwards, he began to practise as a general engineer, for which diligent study during this term had fitted him. He was soon sought after for almost every undertaking of public improvement; whether for the making of bridges, canals, harbours, or any other engineering design projected in Scotland. But the circumstance of a small model of a steam-engine being sent him to repair, fixed his attention powerfully upon the element which had so often excited the attention of his boyish understanding.

Watt found this model so imperfect, although it was the most perfect then known, that he could with difficulty get it to work. The more he examined it, the more deeply he became convinced that the properties of steam had never been understood; the engine was, in fact, an atmospheric rather than a steam engine. By laborious investigation he ascertained that the evaporation of water proceeded more or less rapidly in proportion to the degree of heat made to enter it; that the process of evaporation was quickened as a greater surface of water was exposed to heat, the quantity of coals necessary to raise a certain weight of water into steam, and the degrees of heat at which water boils under different pressures. He had now learnt enough of the nature of the great element he proposed to wield; but it required long thought and the most exhaustless application of contrivance to give his vaporous giant a fitting body, limbs, joints, and sinews, and so to adapt these as to render them a self-regulating mechanism. Watt found a coadjutor in the person of Boulton, of Birmingham, who was possessed of capital, and the will to embark it; and he now set to work to perfect his discovery, and did perfect it; thus revealing to man the greatest instrument of power yet put into his possession.

"In the present perfect state of the engine," says Dr. Arnott, in his "Elements of Physics," "it appears a thing almost endowed with intelligence. It regulates with perfect accuracy and uniformity the number of its strokes in a given time; counting or recording them, moreover, to tell how much work it has done, as a clock records the beats of its pendulum; it regulates the quantity of steam admitted to work; the briskness of the fire; the supply of water to the boiler; the supply of coals to the fire; it opens and shuts its valves with absolute precision as to time and manner; it oils its joints; it takes out any air which may accidentally enter into parts which should be vacuous; and when anything goes wrong, which it cannot itself rectify, it warns its attendants by ringing a bell: yet with all these talents and qualities, and even when exerting the power of six hundred horses, it is obedient to the hand of a child; its aliment is coal, wood, charcoal, or other combustible; it consumes none while idle; it never tires, and wants no sleep; it is not subject to malady when originally well made, and only refuses to work when worn out with age; it is equally active in all climates, and will do work of any kind; it is a water pumper, a miner, a sailor, a cotton-spinner, a weaver, a blacksmith, a miller, &c., &c.; and a small engine, in the character of a steam-pony, may be seen dragging after it on a railroad a hundred tons of merchandise, or a regiment of soldiers, with greater speed than that of our fleetest coaches. It is the king of machines, and a permanent realisation of the genii of Eastern fable, whose supernatural powers were occasionally at the command of man."

And what was the greater instrument? The mind of Watt, whose powers were manifested by the creation of this grandest physical instrument. Could such a display of resources, such amazing circumspection of the wants and needs of his machine, and wisdom in the adaptation of its members to the perfect working of the whole, have been given forth from an intellect untrained itself to rule, uninured itself to toil, and to toil with certitude for an end, by persevering collection of all that could increase its aptitude to reach it? The estimate of James Watt's character by the eloquent Lord Jeffrey, will afford a weighty answer.

"Independently of his great attainments in mechanics, Mr. Watt was an extraordinary, and, in many respects, a wonderful man. Perhaps no individual in his age possessed so much and such varied and exact information—had read so much, or remembered what he had read so accurately and well. He had infinite quickness of apprehension, a prodigious memory, and a certain rectifying and methodising power of understanding, which extracted something precious out of all that was presented to it. His stores of miscellaneous knowledge were immense, and yet less astonishing than the command he had at all times over them. It seemed as if every subject that was casually started in conversation had been that which he had been last occupied in studying and exhausting; such was the copiousness, the precision, the admirable clearness of the information which he poured out upon it without effort or hesitation. Nor was this promptitude and compass of knowledge confined in any degree to the studies connected with his ordinary pursuits. That he should have been minutely and extensively skilled in chemistry and the arts, and in most of the branches of physical science might, perhaps, have been conjectured; but it could not have been inferred from his usual occupations, and, probably, is not generally known, that he was curiously learned in many branches of antiquity, metaphysics, medicine, and etymology, and perfectly at home in all the details of architecture, music, and law. He was well acquainted, too, with most of the modern languages, and familiar with their most recent literature. Nor was it at all extraordinary to hear the great mechanician and engineer detailing and expounding, for hours together, the metaphysical theories of the German logicians, or criticising the measures or the matter of the German poetry.

"His astonishing memory was aided, no doubt, in a great measure, by a still higher and rarer faculty—by his power of digesting and arranging in its proper place all the information he received, and of casting aside and rejecting, as it were instinctively, whatever was worthless or immaterial. Every conception that was suggested to his mind seemed instantly to take its place among its other rich furniture, and to be condensed into the smallest and most convenient form. He never appeared, therefore, to be at all encumbered or perplexed with the *verbiage* of the dull books he perused, or the idle talk to which he listened, but to have at once extracted, by a kind of intellectual alchemy, all that was worthy of attention, and to have reduced it for his own use to its true value and to its simplest form. And thus it often happened that a great deal more was learned, from his brief and vigorous account of the theories and arguments of tedious writers, than an ordinary student could have derived from the most faithful study of the originals; and that errors and absurdities became manifest from the mere clearness and plainness of his statement of them, which might have deluded and perplexed most of his hearers without that invaluable assistance."

Such was the activity, industry, discipline, and perseverance in acquirement, of the mind which gave to the world its greatest physical transformer—the instrument which is changing the entire civilization of the world, "doing the work of multitudes, overcoming the difficulties of depth, distance, minuteness, magnitude, wind, and tide; exhibiting stranger wonders than those of romance or magic; annihilating time and space; giving wings even to thought, and sending knowledge like light through the human universe; most mighty, with power that Watt knew not of, and with more than we know, for futurity. The discovery of America," says the same eloquent writer, W. J. Fox, in his "Lectures to the Working Classes," "was of matter to be worked upon: this is power to work upon the world."

COLUMBUS,

Starts before the mind with the enunciation of the sentence just quoted. He whose indomitable perseverance carried his mutinous sailors onward—and onward—across the dreary Atlantic, in a frail bark, until fidelity to his own convictions issued in the magnificent proof of their verity, the discovery of the new world. But our space demands that we pass to the incomparable name which towers, alone, above that of James Watt, in the world's list of the scientific benefactors of mankind; and, perhaps, above all human names in its peerless excellence.

Return of Columbus.

SIR ISAAC NEWTON,

It is so well known, as scarcely to need repeating here, displayed his wondrous and incontrollable tendency for scientific inquiry in boyhood. In him, too, as in the minds of almost all philosophical discoverers, was evinced the faculty for mechanical contrivance, as well as acuteness for demonstration. The anecdotes of his boyish invention, of his windmill with a mouse for the miller, his water-clock, carriage, and sun-dials, and of his kites and paper lanterns, are familiar. His mother having been persuaded, by an intelligent relative, to give him up from agricultural cares, to which his genius could not be tied down, he was sent to Cambridge, and entered Trinity College in his eighteenth year. He proceeded, at once, to the study of "Descartes' Geometry," regarding "Euclid's Elements" as containing self-evident truths, when he had gone through the titles of the propositions. Yet he afterwards regretted this neglect of the rigid method of demonstration, in the outset, as a great mistake, and wished he had not attached himself so closely to modes of solution by algebra. He successively studied, and wrote commentaries on, "Wallis's Arithmetic of Infinities," "Saunderson's Logic," and "Kepler's Optics;" and, for testing the doctrines of the latter science, bought a prism, and made numerous experiments with it. While but a very young man, Dr. Isaac Barrow, the Lucasian Professor of Mathematics, gathered hints of new truths from his conversation; and in the publication of his lectures on optics, a few years after, the Doctor acknowledged his obligations to young Newton, and characterised him very highly. A year after this publication, Barrow resigned his chair in favour of Newton, who had recently taken the degree of Master of Arts.

Zeal to acquit himself well in his professorship, a situation so congenial to his mind, led him to devote the most profound attention to the doctrines of light and vision. Realities were what he sought, even in the most abstract pursuits; and he expended considerable manual labour in constructing reflecting telescopes. One of these most valued relics of his mechanical toil is now in the library of the Royal Society. The result of his studies and experiments was not fully known before the publication of his "Opticks," in his sixty-second year; but it is believed his entire discovery of the nature of light was made many years before, being at length "put together out of scattered papers." The modesty of this great man was, indeed, the most distinguishing mark of his intellect. Arrogant satisfaction, or pride of superior genius, never sullied his greatness. Even in giving this scientific treasure to the world, he says, he designed to repeat most of his observations with more care and exactness, and to make some new ones for determining the manner how the rays of light are bent in their passage by bodies, for making the fringes of colours with the dark lines between them.

How much are we indebted to the patient perseverance of all the true discoverers in science! This is the quality of mind which ever distinguished them. Rashness and presumption, haste to place his crude theories before the world, and to gain assent to them before proof, on the other hand, are the sure marks of the empiric or pretender. The popular author of "The Pursuit of Knowledge under Difficulties"—a work the young student should carry about with him as a never-failing stimulus to perseverance—thus admirably treats this pre-eminent characteristic of the mind of Newton:— "On some occasions he was wont to say, that, if there was any mental habit or endowment in which he excelled the generality of men, it was that of patience in the examination of the facts and phenomena of his subject. This was merely another form of that teachableness which constituted the character of the man. He loved truth, and wooed her with the unwearying ardour of a lover. Other speculators had consulted the book of nature, principally for the purpose of seeking in it the defence of some favourite theory: partially, therefore, and hastily, as one would consult a dictionary. Newton perused it as a volume altogether worthy of being studied for its own sake. Hence proceeded both the patience with which he traced its characters, and the rich and plentiful discoveries with which the search rewarded him. If he afterwards classified and systematised his knowledge like a philosopher, he had first, to use his own language, gathered it like a child."

This transcendent combination of qualities, modesty, patient investigation, and indefatigable perseverance, was still more wondrously shown in his superlative discovery of the theory of gravitation, than in his promulgation of the laws of light and vision. The anecdote of his observation of the fall of an apple from a tree, while sitting in his garden, is among the most familiar of all anecdotes to general readers. This incident, it was affirmed by his niece, as well as his friend Dr. Pemberton, occurred in Newton's twenty-third year; and it instantly raised in him the inquiry whether the infinite universe were not held in order and kept in motion by the very power which drew the apple to the earth.

Galileo had already shown the tendency of all bodies near the earth to gravitate towards its centre, and had calculated and fixed the proportions of their speed in descent to their distance from the earth's centre. Newton's general application of Galileo's rule to the planets of the solar system led him to regard his conjecture as strongly probable. He next devoted his powers to the consideration of its verity, by examining the question whether the force of gravitation by which the planets preserved their orbits and motions round the sun would precisely account for the moon's preservation of her orbit and motion round the earth. But here the precision of his calculations was frustrated by the imperfect knowledge then existing as to the real measurement of the earth—the gravitating centre of the revolving moon. An empiric would have trumpeted his discovery to the world, in spite of the fact that this faulty admeasurement of the earth, by not affording a true calculation of her gravitating power, failed to lead him to an agreement with truth. Newton was silent for long years, until a degree of the earth's latitude was ascertained, by actual experiment, to be sixty-nine and a half degrees instead of sixty; he then resumed his calculations, and their result was that he had probed the grand secret of the laws by which worlds move in obedience to the suns which are their centres. It only remains to be observed, as a significant reminder to the young reader, that—though he may *assent* to the great doctrine of Newton, and consider it to be established, he can never fully *know* its mathematical and mechanical verity, unless study enables him to read the "Principia"—the work in which the truth of gravitation and its laws are demonstrated. Let it be an additional motive to strive for the ability to read such a book, that in having read it the student has become acquainted with the greatest effort in abstract truth ever yet produced by the human intellect.

The moral as well as the intellectual grandeur of the life of Newton would tempt us to enlarge, but we must merely say, ere we pass on, to the youthful inquirer—read about Newton, think about Newton, and the more you know of him the more will your understanding honour him, your heart love him, and your desire strengthen to approach him in virtue, wisdom, and usefulness.

SIR WILLIAM HERSCHEL,

Newton's greatest successor in astronomical discovery, may claim an equality with him, as a true and noble disciple of perseverance. The son of a poor Hanoverian musician, he was brought over to England, with his father, in the band of the Guards. The father returned to Hanover, but young Herschel remained, and at the age of twenty began to seek his fortune in this country. After many difficulties, wanderings from place to place, as a teacher of music in families, and a few slight glimpses of favour from fortune, he obtained the office of organist in the Octagon Chapel at Bath. The emoluments of this situation, with his receipts from tuition of pupils and other engagements, were such that an ordinary mortal would have been content "to make himself comfortable" upon them, in worldly phrase. But ease and competence were not the object of Herschel's ambition. In the midst of his wanderings, he had not only striven to acquire a sound knowledge of English, but of Italian, Latin, and Greek, and had entered on the study of counterpoint, in order to make himself a profound theorist, as well as a performer, in music. In order to comprehend the doctrines of harmonics, he found it necessary to get some acquaintance with the mathematics; and this led him at once to the line of study for which his natural genius was best fitted. On his settlement at Bath, he applied himself with ardour to these abstract inquiries, and from the mathematics proceeded to astronomy and optics. Desire to view the wonders of the heavens for himself made him eager to possess a telescope; and, deeming the price of a sufficiently powerful one more than he could afford, he set about making a five-feet reflector, and, after much difficulty, accomplished his task.

Success only stimulated him to bolder attempts, and he rapidly constructed telescopes of seven, ten, and twenty-feet focal distance. Pupils and professional engagements were given up, until he reduced his income to a bare sufficiency, in order that he might have more time for the sciences to which he was now become inseparably attached. So tireless was his perseverance in the fashioning of mirrors for his telescopes, that he would sit to polish them for twelve or fourteen hours, without intermission; and, rather than take his hand from the delicate labour, his sister was requested to put the little food he ate into his mouth. With one of his seven-feet reflectors—the most perfect instrument he had constructed—after having been engaged for a year and a half, at intervals, in a regular survey of the heavens, he at length made the discovery of the planet which, until the very recent discovery of "Neptune" by Leverrier and Adams, was regarded as the most distant member of the solar system. The Astronomer-Royal, Dr. Maskelyne, to whom Herschel made known what he had observed, together with his doubts as to the nature of the new celestial body, first affirmed it to be a comet. In a few months this error was dissipated, and the grandeur of Herschel's discovery was acknowledged by the whole scientific world. King George the Third, in whose honour he had named the new planet Georgium Sidus (a name which has been very properly set aside for that of Uranus), conferred upon him a pension of £300 a year, that he might be enabled to give up entirely the profession of music; and the son of the poor Hanoverian musician took his station among the first in the highest of the sciences. The order of knighthood was afterwards bestowed upon him; but it could not add to the splendour of the names of either Herschel or Newton.

Inquiry will put the young reader in possession of a knowledge of many other interesting and important discoveries of the *persevering* Herschel. A few pages must be devoted to a brief mention of others who have benefited mankind by their unremitting labours; and they must be selected from a list where it is difficult to tell a single name unmarked by some peculiar excellence—so abundant in exemplars of meritorious toil is the vast muster-roll of science and mechanical invention.

REAUMUR,

May be instanced as one of the most industrious toilers for the advancement of useful science, though he does not take rank with the unfolders of sublime truths. During a life of seventy-five years he was incessantly engaged in endeavouring to add something to the compass of human knowledge and convenience. At one time he is found pursuing an investigation into the mode of formation and growth of shells, endeavouring to account for the progressive motion of the different kinds of testaceous animals; anon, he publishes a "Natural History of Cobwebs," evincing a mind capable of the most minute and ingenious search; and is afterwards found showing the facility with which iron and steel may be made magnetic by percussion. For revealing to his countrymen, the French, a method of converting forged or bar-iron into steel, of making steel of what quality they pleased, and of rendering even cast-iron ductile, a pension of twelve hundred livres yearly was settled upon him. This allowance, at his death, was settled, by his own request, on the Academy of Sciences, to be applied to the defraying of expenses for future attempts to improve the arts. He also made known the useful secret of tinning plates of iron, an article for which the French, till his time, had been compelled to resort to Germany.

Continuing his researches into natural science, he showed the means by which marine animals attach themselves to solid bodies; discussed the cause of the electric effect from the stroke of a torpedo; displayed the proof that in crabs, lobsters, and crayfish, nature reproduces a lost claw; set forth a treatise showing, by experiments, that the digestive process is performed in granivorous birds by trituration, and in carnivorous by solution; and published a systematic "History of Insects." Engaged at one period of life in proving, by experiment, that the less a cord is twisted the stronger it is—that is, that the best mode of uniting the threads of a cord is that which causes their tension to be equal in whatever direction the cord is strained; we find him, at another period, discovering the art of preserving eggs, so that they might be kept fresh and fit for incubation many years, and breeds of fowls propagated at home or abroad, by the eggs being washed with a varnish of oil, grease, or any other substance that would effectually stop the pores of the shell, and prevent the contents from evaporating. Valuable secrets in the making of glass were also discovered by him; he devised a method of making porcelain, and showed that the requisite materials were to be found in France in greater abundance than in the East; and lastly, he rendered enduring service to science by reducing thermometers to a common standard, which continental nations gratefully commemorate by still calling thermometers by his name. A life passed in mental occupations so multifarious as well as useful, surely entitles Reaumur to be termed a true scholar of perseverance.

THE HONOURABLE ROBERT BOYLE,

By a life of virtue and usefulness, merits the epithet to which his birth by courtesy entitled him. He was the youngest son of the first Earl of Cork, and after being educated at Eton was sent out to travel on the continent. A residence at Florence at the time of Galileo's death, and the almost universal conversation then caused by the discoveries of that great philosopher, seem to have induced Boyle's first attention to science. On returning to this country he very soon joined a knot of scientific men, who had begun to meet at each other's houses, on a certain day in each week, for inquiry and discussion into what was then called "The New or Experimental Philosophy." These weekly meetings eventually gave rise to the Royal Society of London; but part of the original members of the little club, a few years after its commencement, removed to Oxford, and Boyle, influenced by his attachment to these philosophic friends, in process of time took up his residence in that city. Their weekly meetings were held in his house; and here he began to prosecute with earnestness his researches into the nature of air. By his experiments and invention, the air-pump was first brought into so useful a form that he may be called its discoverer, though the genius of others has since greatly improved that important instrument. He also demonstrated the necessity of the presence of air for the support of animal life and of combustion; showing not only that a flame is instantly extinguished beneath an exhausted receiver, but that even a fish could not live under it, though immersed in water. His demonstration of the expansibility of air was still more important. Aristotle, three hundred years before the Christian era, taught that if air were rarefied till it filled ten times its usual space, it would become fire. Boyle succeeded in dilating a portion of the air of the common atmosphere, till it filled nearly fourteen thousand times its natural space.

His other discoveries were numerous, every hour of his existence might be said to be devoted to usefulness: and his wealth and station, so far from disposing him to ease and inertion, were nobly turned by him into grand aids for the advancement of knowledge. Mr. Craik thus admirably sums up his life of effort:—"From his boyhood till his death he may be said to have been almost constantly occupied in making philosophical experiments; collecting and ascertaining facts in natural science; inventing or improving instruments for the examination of nature; maintaining a regular correspondence with scientific men in all parts of Europe; receiving the daily visits of great numbers of the learned, both of his own and other countries; perusing and studying not only all the new works that appeared in the large and rapidly widening department of natural history and mathematical and experimental physics, including medicine, anatomy, chemistry, geography, &c., but many others, relating especially to theology and oriental literature; and, lastly, writing so profusely upon all these subjects, that those of his works alone which have been preserved and collected, independently of many others that are lost, fill, in one edition, six large quarto volumes. So vast an amount of literary performance, from a man who was at the same time so much of a public character, and gave so considerable a portion of his time to the service of others, shows strikingly what may be done by industry, *perseverance*, and such a method of life as never suffers an hour of the day to run to waste."

The lives of Copernicus, Tycho Brahe, Galileo, and Kepler, among astronomers; of Napier of Murchiston, the inventor of logarithms; of Dolland and Ramsden, the improvers of optical glasses; of Cavendish, the discoverer of the composition of water; of Linnæus and Cuvier, the greatest naturalists; of Lavoisier, Fourcroy, Black, and, indeed, a host of modern chemists; might be singly and in order adduced as inspiring lessons of perseverance. The young inquirer, if he have caught a spark of zeal from the ardour of the tireless minds we have hastily endeavoured to portray, will, if he act worthily, strive to make himself acquainted more fully with the doings of these and other great men, and "gird up the loins of his mind" to follow them in their glorious path of wisdom and beneficence.

CHAPTER VI.
MEN OF BUSINESS.

Examples of a successful pursuit of wealth, either from the beginnings of a moderate fortune, or from absolute penury, are abundant. A life devoted to the acquirement of money, for its own sake, cannot be made the subject of moral eulogy; it can only be introduced among the "Triumphs of Perseverance," as a proof of the efficacy of that quality of the mind to enable the wealth-winner to compass his resolves. It by no means follows, however, that a career towards opulence is impelled by the mere sordid passion for gain. Happily, among those who have started with a moderate fortune, progressive increase in riches has often been found united with increasing purposes of the noblest philanthropy and public beneficence; while the manly aim for independence has equally distinguished many who have risen to wealth from poverty. A brief rehearsal of the biographies of two persons, of widely different station and character, but whose names have alike become inseparably connected with the history of the first commercial city in the world, will suffice to illustrate our position.

SIR THOMAS GRESHAM,

The younger son of Sir Richard, who was a knight, alderman, sheriff, and Lord Mayor of London, and a prosperous merchant, had the twofold example set him by his father, of an intelligent pursuit of trade, and of public spirit and munificence. He was sent to Cambridge, distinguished himself in study, and might, undoubtedly, have risen to reputation in one of the learned professions; but, by his father's wish, he turned his attention to business, and was admitted a member of the Mercers' Company at the age of twenty-four. Having, through his father's eminence as a merchant, succeeded in obtaining the trust of agent to King Edward the Sixth, for taking up money of the merchants of Antwerp, he quickly discerned the abuses under which the king's interest suffered. He proposed methods for preventing the Flemish merchants from extorting unfair commissions and brokages, and so turned the current of advantage to the king's favour, that the young prince was enabled to pay all the debts for which his father and the Protector—Somerset—had left him responsible. During the short reign of Edward, this active and enterprising merchant made forty journeys from England to Antwerp; and, by the application of his genius, retrieved English commerce from the disadvantage into which it had fallen by mismanagement at home, and the superior shrewdness of the Netherland merchants. The precious metals had become scarce in our country, but Gresham brought them back again; our commodities were low in price, and foreign ones high, but he reversed their conditions of sale: while the king's credit, from being very low abroad, was, by Gresham's skill, raised so high, that he could have borrowed what sums he pleased. For such services the young and acute negotiator had a pension of £100 a year appointed him for life, and estates to the value of £300 a year were also conferred upon him by the king.

At the accession of Mary, Gresham was discharged from his agency; but, on his drawing up a memorial, and its allegements being proved, he was re-instated. Queen Elizabeth immediately re-engaged him, at her accession, and employed him to provide and buy up arms for the national defence. She knighted him a year afterwards, and he then built himself the mansion known by his name in Bishopsgate Street; and, till lately, occupied by the "Gresham professors."

His noblest public work was performed soon after. His father had striven to move King Henry the Eighth to build an Exchange for the city merchants, who then met in the open air in Lombard Street, but could not. Sir Thomas Gresham now publicly proposed, if the citizens would purchase a piece of ground large enough, and in the proper place, to build an Exchange at his own expense, with covered walks, and all necessary conveniences for the assemblage of merchants. This was done; the site was cleared; Gresham himself laid the foundation stone; and Queen Elizabeth, when the building was complete, "attended by nobility, came from Somerset House, and caused it, by trumpet and herald, to be proclaimed the 'Royal Exchange.'" This building, as our young readers know, was burnt down some years ago, and the present stately fabric, opened by Queen Victoria, has been erected on its site.

About the time that the building of the Royal Exchange was commenced, Gresham was again employed to take up moneys for the royal use at Antwerp. Experience had so fully shown him the evil of pursuing this system, that he at length persuaded the Queen to discontinue it, and to borrow of her own merchants in the city of London. Yet his views were so much in advance of the contracted commercial spirit of that age, that the London citizens, in their common hall, blind to their own interests, negatived his proposition when it was first made to them. But, on more mature consideration, several merchants and aldermen raised £16,000, and lent it to the Queen for six months, at six per cent. interest; and the loan was prolonged for six months more, at the same interest, with brokage. This illustrious London citizen, by his superior intelligence, thus opened the way for increasing others' as well as his own gains.

Sir Thomas Gresham's successful negotiations issued in so large an increase of his own wealth, that he purchased large estates in several counties, and bought Osterley Park, near Brentford, where he built a large mansion, in which he was accustomed to receive the visits of Elizabeth. Even here the ideas of the merchant were predominant. "The house," says a writer of the period, "standeth in a parke, well wooded and garnished with many faire ponds, which affoorded not onely fish and fowle, as swannes and other water fowle, but also great use for milles, as paper milles, oyle milles, and corn milles." On his retirement to Osterley, he transformed his residence in Bishopsgate Street into a "college," for the abode of seven bachelor professors, who were to read lectures there on "divinity, law, physic, astronomy, geometry, music, and rhetoric," and to have £50 each per year.

He was the richest commoner in England—such were what is usually termed "the substantial" rewards of his perseverance; while his name deserves lasting honour as the patron of learning, and the exemplar of merchant-beneficence. He left, by will, not only ample funds for continuing his "professorships," but endowments for almshouses, and yearly sums for ten of the city prisons and hospitals.

JAMES LACKINGTON,

The son of a journeyman shoemaker and of a weaver's daughter, passed his early years amidst circumstances which must have enduringly impressed him with the miseries of vice and poverty. His father was a selfish and habitual drunkard, and his mother frequently worked nineteen or twenty hours out of the four-and-twenty to support her family. He was the eldest child of a numerous family, and was put two or three years to a dame's school; but was less intent on learning than on "getting on in the world," even while a boy. He heard a pieman cry his wares, and soon proposed to a baker to sell pies for him; and so successful did young Lackington prove as a pie-vender, that he heard the baker declare, a twelvemonth after, that he had been the means of extricating him from embarrassment. A boyish prank put an end to this engagement; and when the baker wished to renew it Lackington's father insisted on placing him at the stall. Again, however, his pedlar inclinations, which in after life led him to affluence, rescued him from the disagreeable treatment he expected to receive under his father's rule. He heard a man cry almanacks in the street, and importuned his father till he obtained leave to start on the same itinerant enterprise. In this he succeeded so well that he deeply aggrieved the other venders, who, as he tells us in his very whimsical but interesting biography, would have "done him a mischief had he not possessed a light pair of heels." Resolute on not continuing at home, he persuaded his father, at length, to bind him apprentice with a shoemaker in a neighbouring town, and at fourteen years of age sat down to learn his trade.

We will not follow this singular specimen of human nature, spoilt by want of education and by evil example, through all the vagaries of his youth. Taking him up at four-and-twenty, after he had experienced considerable changes in religious feeling, and gathered some smatterings of knowledge from reading, we find him marrying, and beginning the world the next morning with one halfpenny. Yet he and his wife set cheerfully to work, he tells us; and by great industry and self-denial, they not only earned a living, but paid off a debt of forty shillings, which was somewhat summarily claimed by a friend of whom he had borrowed that sum. Trials very soon fell to his lot which tended to make him deeply thoughtful. His wife was ill for six months; and, at the end of that period, he was compelled to remove her from Bristol to Taunton, for her health's sake. During two years and a half the poor woman was removed five times to and from Taunton without permanent recovery; and Lackington, despairing of an amendment of his circumstances under such discouragements, resolved to leave his native district. He therefore gave his wife all the money he had, except what he thought would suffice to bring him to London; and, mounting a stage coach, reached town with but half-a-crown in his pocket. He got work the next morning, saved enough in a month to bring up his wife, and she had tolerable health, and obtained "binding work" from his employer.

Lackington was now fairly entered on the path to prosperity. His partner was a pattern of self-denial and economy; they began to save money, bought clothes, and then household furniture, left lodgings, and had a house of their own. A friend, not long after, proposed that Lackington should take a little shop and parlour, which were "to let" in Featherstone-street, City-road, and commence master shoemaker. Lackington agreed, but also formed the resolution to sell old books. With his own scanty collection, a bagful of old volumes he purchased for a guinea, and his scraps of leather, altogether worth about 5*l*, he accordingly commenced master tradesman. He soon sold off, and increased his stock of books; and next borrowed 5*l* of John Wesley's people—"a sum of money kept on purpose to lend out for three months, without interest, to such of their society whose characters were good, and who wanted temporary relief." Much to his shame he traduces the character of the philanthropic Wesley and of his brother religionists, in his "Confessions," even while acknowledging that this benevolent loan was "of great service" to him. He afterwards endeavoured to make the *amende honorable*, but the mode in which it was made was as unadmirable as his ungrateful offence. But, to return to his narrative.

"In our new situation," says he, "we lived in a very frugal manner, often dining on potatoes, and quenching our thirst with water, being determined, if possible, to make some provision for such dismal times as sickness and shortness of work, which had often been our lot, and might be again." In six months he became worth five-and-twenty pounds in old book stock, removed into Chiswell-street, to a more commodious shop, though the street, he says, was then (in 1775) a dull street, gave up shoemaking, "turned his leather into books," and soon began to have a great sale. Another series of reverses, during which his wife died, his shop was closed, while he himself was prostrate with fever, and was robbed by nurses, only served to sharpen his intents and strengthen his perseverance, when he recovered. His second marriage, with an intelligent woman, he found of immense advantage, since his new partner was a very efficient helpmate in the book-shop. Next, his friend Dennis became partaker in his business, and advanced a small capital, by which they "doubled stock," and printed their first catalogue of 12,000 volumes. They took 20*l.* the first week, and Dennis then advanced 200*l.* more towards the trade; but, after two years, Lackington was left once more to himself, his friend being weary of the business. A resolution not to give credit gave him great difficulty, he says, for at least seven years, but he carried his plan at last, principally by selling at very small profits. His business premises were successively enlarged, and his sales likewise, until his trade and himself became wonders. At the age of fifty-two he went out of business, leaving his cousin head of the firm. He sold 100,000 volumes annually, during the latter years of his personal attention to trade, kept his carriage, purchased two estates, and built himself a genteel house. He once more became a professor of religion, on retiring from business, and built several chapels. He was, in the close of life, benevolent in visiting the sick and indigent, and in relieving the distressed.

"As the first king of Bohemia kept his country shoes by him to remind him from whence he was taken," says the bookseller, in his "Confessions," "so I have put a motto on the doors of my carriage, constantly to remind me to what I am indebted for my prosperity, viz. 'Small profits do great things;' and reflecting on the means by which I have been enabled to support a carriage, adds not a little to the pleasure of riding in it." Alluding to the stories that were rife respecting his success, attributing it to his purchasing a "fortunate lottery-ticket," or "finding bank-notes in an old book," he says, very emphatically, "I found the whole that I am possessed of, in—*small profits*, bound by *industry*, and clasped by *economy*."

CHAPTER VII.
PHILANTHROPISTS.

One conviction forms the basis of all correct admiration for the heroism and intrepidity of scientific discoverers, the marvellous inventions of mechanicians; the sublime enthusiasm of poets, artists, and musicians; the laborious devotion of scholars; and even of the intelligent industry of the accumulators of wealth: it is that all their efforts and achievements tend, by the law of our nature, to the amelioration of man's condition. In every mind swayed by reflection, and not by impulse or prejudice, the world's admiration for warriors is regarded as mistaken, because the deeds of the soldier are the infliction of suffering and destruction, spring from the most evil passions, and serve but to keep up the real hindrances of civilization and human happiness. Statues and columns erected in honour of conquerors, excellent as they may be for the display of art, serve, therefore, in every correct mind, for subjects of regretful rather than encouraging and satisfactory contemplation. The self-sacrificing enterprises of the philanthropist, on the contrary, create in every properly regulated mind, still purer admiration, still more profound and enduring esteem, than even the noblest and grandest efforts of the children of Mind and Imagination. The DIVINE EXEMPLAR himself is at the head of their class; and they seem, of all the sons of men, most transcendently to reflect his image, because their deeds are direct acts of mercy and goodness, and misery and suffering flee at their approach. Harbingers of the benign reign of Human Brotherhood which the popular spirit of our age devoutly regards as the eventual destiny of the world, they will be venerated, and their memories cherished and loved, when laurelled conquerers are mentioned no more with praise, or are forgotten. Emulation is sometimes termed a motive of questionable morality; but to emulate the high and holy in enterprises of self-sacrificing beneficence can never be an unworthy passion; for half the value of a good man's life would be lost, if his example did not serve to fill others with such a plenitude of love for his goodness, as to impel them to imitate him.

It is the example of the philanthropist, then, that we commend, above all other examples, to the imitation of all who are beginning life. We would say, scorn indolence, ignorance, and reckless imprudence that makes you dependent on others' effort instead of your own; but, more than all, scorn selfishness and a life useless to man, your brother, cleave to knowledge, industry, and refinement; but, beyond all, cleave to goodness.

In a world where so much is wrong—where, for ages, the cupidity of some, and the ignorance and improvidence of a greater number—has increased the power of wrong, it need not be said how dauntless must be the soul of perseverance needed to overcome this wrong by the sole and only effectual efforts of gentleness and goodness. That wisdom—deeply calculating wisdom—not impulsive and indiscriminate "charity," as it is falsely named—should also lend its calm but energetic guidance to him who aims to assist in removing the miseries of the world, must be equally evident. To understand to what morally resplendent deeds this dauntless spirit can conduct, when thus guided by wisdom, and armed with the sole power of gentleness, we need to fix our observance but on one name—the most worshipful soldier of humanity our honoured land has ever produced: the true champion of *persevering* goodness.

JOHN HOWARD,

Inheriting a handsome competence from his father, whom he lost while young, went abroad early, and in Italy acquired a taste for art. He made purchases of such specimens of the great masters as his means would allow, and embellished therewith his paternal seat of Cardington, in Bedfordshire. His first wife, who had attended him with the utmost kindness during a severe illness, and whom, though much older than himself, he had married from a principle of gratitude, died within three years of their union; and to relieve his mind from the melancholy occasioned by her death, he resolved on leaving England for another tour. The then recent earthquake which had laid Lisbon in ruins, rendered Portugal a clime of interest with him, and he set sail for that country. The packet, however, was captured by a French privateer; and he and other prisoners were carried into Brest, and placed in the castle. They had been kept forty hours without food or water before entering the filthy dungeon into which they were cast, and it was still a considerable time before a joint of mutton was thrown into the midst of them, which, for want of the accommodation even of a solitary knife, they were obliged to tear to pieces and gnaw like dogs. For nearly a week Howard and his companions were compelled to lie on the floor of this dungeon, with nothing but straw to shelter them from its noxious and unwholesome damps. He was then removed to another town where British prisoners were kept; and though permitted to reside in the town on his "parole," or word of honour, he had evidence, he says, that many hundreds of his countrymen perished in their imprisonment, and that, at one place, thirty-six were buried in a hole in one day. He was at length permitted to return home, but it was upon his promise to go back to France, if his own government should refuse to exchange him for a French naval officer. As he was only a private individual, it was doubtful whether government would consent to this; and he desired his friends to forbear the congratulations with which they welcomed his return, assuring them he should perform his promise, if government expressed a refusal. Happily the negotiation terminated favourably, and Howard felt himself, once more, at complete freedom in his native land.

It is to this event, comprising much personal suffering for himself, and the grievous spectacle of so much distress endured by his sick and dying fellow-countrymen in bonds, that the first great emotion in the mind of this exalted philanthropist must be dated. Yet, like many deep thoughts which have resulted in noble actions, Howard's grand life-thought lay a long time in the germ within the recesses of his reflective faculty. He first returned to his Cardington estate, and, together with his delight in the treasures of art, occupied his mind with meteorological observations, which he followed up with such assiduity as to draw upon himself some notice from men of science, and to be chosen a Fellow of the Royal Society.

After his second marriage, he continued to reside upon his estate, and to improve and beautify it. The grounds were, indeed, laid out with a degree of taste only equalled on the estates of the nobility. But it was impossible for such a nature as Howard's to be occupied solely with a consideration of his pleasures and comforts. His tenantry were the constant objects of his care, and in the improvement of their habitations and modes of life he found delightful employment for by far the greater portion of his time. In his beneficent plans for the amelioration of the condition of the poor he was nobly assisted by the second Mrs. Howard, who was a woman of exemplary and self-sacrificing benevolence. One act alone affords delightful proof of this. She sold her jewels soon after her marriage, and put the money into a purse called, by herself and her husband, "the charity-purse," from the consecration of its contents to the relief of the poor and destitute.

The death of this excellent woman plunged him again into sorrow, from which he, at first, sought relief in watching over the nurture of the infant son she had left him, having breathed her last soon after giving birth to the child. When his son was old enough to be transferred entirely to the care of a tutor, Howard renewed his visits to the continent. His journal contains proof that his mind was deeply engaged in reflection on all he saw; but neither yet does the master-thought of his life appear to have strengthened to such a degree as to make itself very evident in the workings of his heart and understanding. His election to the office of high sheriff of the county of Bedford, on his return, seems to have been the leading occurrence in his life, judging by the influence it threw on the tone of his thinkings and the character of his acts, to the end of his mortal career. He was forty-six years of age at the time of his election to this office, intellectual culture had refined his character, and much personal trial and affliction had deepened his experience: the devotion of such a man as John Howard to his great errand of philanthropy was not, therefore, any vulgar and merely impulsive enthusiasm. We have seen that the germ of his design had lain for years in his mind, scarcely fructifying or unfolding itself, except in the kindly form of homely charity. The power was now about to be breathed upon it which should quicken it into the mightiest energy of human goodness.

He thus records the grievances he now began to grow ardent for removing: "The distress of prisoners, of which there are few who have not some imperfect idea, came more immediately under my notice when I was sheriff of the county of Bedford; and the circumstance which excited me to activity in their behalf was, the seeing some, who by the verdict of juries were declared *not guilty*—some, on whom the grand jury did not find such an appearance of guilt as subjected them to trial—and some whose prosecutors did not appear against them—after having been confined for months, dragged back to gaol, and locked up again till they could pay *sundry fees* to the gaoler, the clerk of assize, &c. In order to redress this hardship, I applied to the justices of the county for a salary to the gaoler in lieu of his fees. The bench were properly affected with the grievance, and willing to grant the relief desired; but they wanted a precedent for charging the county with the expense. I therefore rode into several neighbouring counties in search of a precedent; but I soon learned that the same injustice was practised in them; and looking into the prisons, I beheld scenes of calamity which I grew daily more and more anxious to alleviate." How free from violence of emotion and exaggerated expression is his statement; how calmly, rationally, and thoughtfully he commenced his glorious enterprise!

He commences, soon after this, a series of journeys for the inspection of English prisons; and visits, successively, the gaols of Cambridge, Huntingdon, Northampton, Leicester, Nottingham, Derby, Stafford, Warwick, Worcester, Gloucester, Oxford, and Buckingham. In many of the gaols he found neither court-yard, water, beds, nor even straw, for the use of the prisoners: no sewers, most miserable provisions, and those extremely scanty, and the whole of the rooms gloomy, filthy, and loathsome. The greatest oppressions and cruelties were practised on the wretched inmates: they were heavily ironed for trivial offences, and frequently confined in dungeons under ground. The Leicester gaol presented more inhuman features than any other; the free ward for debtors who could not afford to pay for better accommodation, was a long dungeon called a cellar, down seven steps—damp, and having but two windows in it, the largest about a foot square; the rooms in which the felons were confined night and day were also dungeons from five to seven steps under ground.

In the course of another tour he visited the gaols of Hertford, Berkshire, Wiltshire, Dorsetshire, Hampshire, and Sussex; set out again to revisit the prisons of the Midlands; spent a fortnight in viewing the gaols of London and Surrey; and then went once more on the same great errand of mercy into the west of England. Shortly after his return he was examined before a Committee of the whole House of Commons, gave full and satisfactory answers to the questions proposed to him, and was then called before the bar of the House to receive from the Speaker the assurance "that the House were very sensible of the humanity and zeal which had led him to visit the several gaols of this kingdom, and to communicate to the House the interesting observations he had made upon that subject."

The intention of the Legislature to proceed to the correction of prison abuses, which the noble philanthropist might infer from this expression of thanks, did not cause him to relax in the pursuit of the high mission he was now so earnestly entered upon. After examining thoroughly the shameless abuses of the Marshalsea, in London, he proceeded to Durham, from thence through Northumberland, Cumberland, Westmoreland, and Lancashire, and inspected not only the prisons in those counties, but a third time went through the degraded gaols of the Midlands. A week's rest at Cardington, and away he departs to visit the prisons in Kent, and to examine all he had not yet entered in London. North and South Wales and the gaols of Chester, and again Worcester and Oxford, he next surveys, and discovers another series of subjects for the exertion of his benevolence.

"Seeing," says he, in his uniform and characteristic vein of modesty, "in two or three of the *county gaols* some poor creatures whose aspect was singularly deplorable, and asking the cause of it, I was answered they were lately brought from the *Bridewells*. This started a fresh subject of inquiry. I resolved to inspect the Bridewells; and for that purpose I travelled again into the counties where I had been, and indeed into all the rest, examining *houses of correction and city and town gaols*. I beheld in many of them, as well as in county gaols, a complication of distress; but my attention was particularly fixed by the gaol-fever and small-pox which I saw prevailing to the destruction of multitudes, not only of felons in their dungeons, but of debtors also." His holy mission now comprehended for the philanthropist the enterprise of lessening the disease as well as unjust and inhuman treatment of prisoners.

The most striking scene of wrong detailed in any of his narratives is in the account of the "Clink" prison of Plymouth, a part of the town gaol. This place was seventeen feet by eight, and five feet and a half high. It was utterly dark, and had no air except what could be derived through an extremely small wicket in the door. To this wicket, the dimensions of which were about seven inches by five, three prisoners under sentence of transportation came by turns to breathe, being confined in that wretched hole for nearly two months.

When Howard visited this place the door had not been opened for five weeks. With considerable difficulty he entered, and with deeply wounded feelings beheld an emaciated human being, the victim of barbarity, who had been confined there ten weeks. This unfortunate creature, who was under sentence of transportation, declared to the humane visitor who thus risked his health and was happy to forego ease and comfort to relieve the oppressed sufferer, that he would rather have been hanged than thrust into that loathsome dungeon.

The electors of Bedford, two years after Howard had held the shrievalty of their county, urged him to become a candidate for the representation of their borough in Parliament. He gave a reluctant consent, but through unfair dealing was unsuccessful. We may, for a moment, regret that the great philanthropist was not permitted to introduce into the Legislature of England measures for the relief of the oppressed suggested by his own large sympathies and experience; but it was far better that he was freed from the shackles of attendance on debates, and spared for ministration not only to the sufferings of the injured in England but in Europe.

He had long purposed to give to the world in a printed form the result of his laborious investigations into the state of prisons in this country; but "conjecturing," he says, "that something useful to his purpose might be collected abroad, he laid aside his papers and travelled into France, Flanders, Holland, and Germany." We have omitted to state that he had already visited many of the prisons in Scotland and Ireland. At Paris he gained admission to some of the prisons with extreme difficulty; but to get access to the state prisons the jealousy of the governments rendered it almost impossible, and under any circumstances dangerous. The intrepid heart of Howard, however, was girt up to adventure, and he even dared to attempt an entrance into the infamous Bastille itself! "I knocked hard," he says, "at the outer gate, and immediately went forward through the guard to the drawbridge before the entrance of the castle; but while I was contemplating this gloomy mansion, an officer came out of the castle much surprised, and I was forced to retreat through the mute guard, and thus regained that freedom, which, for one locked up within those walls, it would be next to impossible to obtain." In the space of four centuries, from the foundation to the destruction of the Bastille, it has been observed that Howard was the only person ever compelled to quit it with reluctance.

By taking advantage of some regulations of the Paris Parliament, he succeeded in gaining admission to other prisons, and found even greater atrocities committed there than in the very worst gaols in England. Flanders presented a striking contrast. "However rigorous they may be," says he, speaking of the regulations for the prisons of Brussels, "yet their great care and attention to their prisons is worthy of commendation: all fresh and clean, no gaol distemper, no prisoners ironed. The bread allowance far exceeds that of any of our gaols; every prisoner here has two pounds of bread per day, soup once every day, and on Sunday one pound of meat." He notes afterwards that he "carefully visited some Prussian, Austrian, and Hessian gaols," and "with the utmost difficulty" gained access to "many dismal abodes" of prisoners.

Returning to England, he travelled through every county repursuing his mission, and after devoting three months to a renewed inspection of the London prisons again set out for the continent. Our space will not allow of a record of the numerous evils he chronicles in these renewed visits. The prisoners of Switzerland, but more than all, of Holland, afforded him a relief to the vision of horrors he witnessed elsewhere. We must find room for some judicious observations he makes on his return from this tour. "When I formerly made the tour of Europe," are his words, "I seldom had occasion to envy foreigners anything I saw with respect to their *situation*, their *religion*, *manners*, or *government*. In my late journeys to view their *prisons* I was sometimes put to the blush for my native country. The reader will scarcely feel, from my narration, the same emotions of shame and regret as the comparison excited in me on beholding the difference with my own eyes; but from the account I have given him of foreign prisons, he may judge whether a design for reforming their own be merely visionary—whether *idleness*, *debauchery*, *disease*, and *famine*, be the necessary attendants of a prison, or only connected with it in our ideas for want of a more perfect knowledge and more enlarged views. I hope, too, that he will do me the justice to think that neither an indiscriminate admiration of every thing foreign, nor a fondness for censuring every thing at home, has influenced me to adopt the language of a panegyrist in this part of my work, or that of a complainant in the rest. Where I have commended I have mentioned my reasons for so doing; and I have dwelt, perhaps, more minutely upon the management of foreign prisons because it was more agreeable to praise than to condemn. Another motive induced me to be very particular in my accounts of *foreign houses of correction*, especially those of the freest states. It was to counteract a notion prevailing among us that compelling prisoners to work, especially in public, was inconsistent with the principles of English liberty; at the same time that taking away the lives of such numbers, either by executions or the diseases of our prisons, seems to make little impression upon us; of such force are custom and prejudice in silencing the voice of good sense and humanity. I have only to add that, fully sensible of the imperfections which must attend the cursory survey of a traveller, it was my study to remedy that defect by a constant attention to the one object of my pursuit alone during the whole of my two last journeys abroad."

He did not allow himself a single day's rest on returning to England, but immediately recommenced his work here. He notes some pleasing improvements, particularly in the Nottingham gaol, since his last preceding visit; but narrates other discoveries of a most revolting description. The gaol at Knaresborough was in the ruined castle, and had but two rooms without a window. The keeper lived at a distance, there being no accommodation for him in the prison. The debtors' gaol was horrible; it consisted of only one room difficult of access, had an earthen floor, no fire-place, and there was a common sewer from the town running through it uncovered! In this miserable and disgusting hole Howard learned that an officer had been confined some years before, who took with him his dog to defend him from vermin: his face was, however, much disfigured by their attacks, and the dog was actually destroyed by them.

At length he prepared to print his "State of the Prisons of England and Wales, with preliminary observations, and an Account of some Foreign Prisons." In this laborious and valuable work, he was largely assisted by the excellent Dr. Aikin, a highly congenial mind; and it was completed in a form which, even in a literary point of view, makes it valuable. The following very brief extract from it, is full of golden reflection: "Most gentlemen who, when they are told of the misery which our prisoners suffer, content themselves with saying, '*Let them take care to keep out*,' prefaced, perhaps, with an angry prayer, seem not duly sensible of the favour of Providence, which distinguishes them from the sufferers: they do not remember that we are required to imitate our gracious Heavenly Parent, who is '*kind to the unthankful and the evil*.' They also forget the vicissitudes of human affairs; the unexpected changes, to which all men are liable; and that those whose circumstances are affluent, may, in time, be reduced to indigence, and become debtors and prisoners."

As soon as his book was published he presented copies of it to most of the principal persons in the kingdom,—thus devoting his wealth, in another form, to the cause of humanity. When it is recounted that he had not only spent large sums in almost incessant travelling, during four years, but had paid the prison fees of numbers who could not otherwise have been liberated, although their periods of sentence had transpired, some idea may be formed of the heart that was within this great devotee of mercy and goodness—the purest of all worships.

The spirits of all reflecting men were roused by this book: the Parliament passed an act for the better regulation of the "hulk" prisons; and on Howard's visiting the hulks and detecting the evasions practised by the superintendents, the government proceeded to rectify the abuses. Learning that government projected further prison reforms, he again set out for the continent to gain additional information in order to lay it before the British

Parliament. An accident at the Hague confined him to his room for six weeks, by throwing him into an inflammatory fever; but he was no sooner recovered than he proceeded to enter on his work anew, by visiting the prison at Rotterdam,—departing thence through Osnaburgh and Hanover, into Germany, Prussia, Bohemia, Austria, Italy, Switzerland, and back through France, again reaching England. Not to enumerate any of his statements respecting his prison visits, let us point the young reader to the answer he gave to Prince Henry of Prussia, who, in the course of his first conversation with the earnest philanthropist, asked him whether he ever went to any public place in the evening, after the labours of the day were over. "Never," he replied, "as I derive more pleasure from doing my duty than from any amusement whatever." What a thorough putting-on of the great martyr spirit there was in the life of this pure-souled man!

Listen, too, to the evidence of his careful employment of the faculty of reason, while thus enthusiastically devoted to the tenderest offices of humanity: "I have frequently been asked what precautions I used to preserve myself from infection in the prisons and hospitals which I visit. I here answer once for all, that next to the free goodness and mercy of the Author of my being, temperance and cleanliness are my preservatives. Trusting in Divine Providence, and being myself in the way of my duty, I visit the most noxious cells, and while thus employed '*I fear no evil*' I never enter an hospital or prison before breakfast, and in an offensive room I seldom draw my breath deeply."

Mark his intrepid championship of Truth, too, as well as of Mercy. He was dining at Vienna, with the English ambassador to the Austrian court, and one of the ambassador's party, a German, had been uttering some praises of the Emperor's abolition of torture. Howard declared it was only to establish a worse torture, and instanced an Austrian prison which, he said, was "as bad as the black hole at Calcutta," and that prisoners were only taken from it when they confessed what was laid to their charge. "Hush!" said the English ambassador (Sir Robert Murray Keith), "your words will be reported to his Majesty!" "What!" exclaimed Howard, "shall my tongue be tied from speaking truth by any king or emperor in the world? I repeat what I asserted, and maintain its veracity." Profound silence ensued, and "every one present," says Dr. Brown, "admired the intrepid boldness of the man of humanity."

Another return to England, another survey of prisons here, and he sets out on his fourth continental tour of humanity, travelling through Denmark, Sweden, Russia, Poland, and then, again, Holland and Germany. Another general and complete revisitation of prisons in England followed, and then a fifth continental pilgrimage of goodness through Portugal, Spain, France, the Netherlands, and Holland. During his absence from England this time, his friends proposed to erect a monument to him; but he was gloriously great in humility as in truth, benevolence, and intrepidity. "Oh, why could not my friends," says he, in writing to them, "who know how much I detest such parade, have stopped such a hasty measure?... It deranges and confounds all my schemes. My exaltation is my fall—my misfortune."

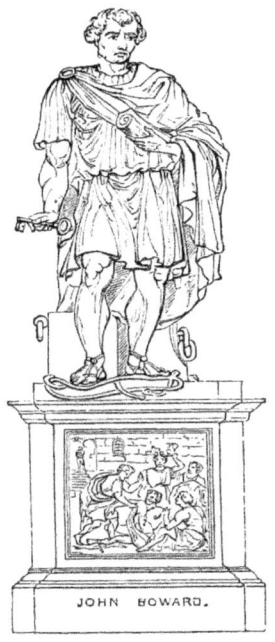

JOHN HOWARD.

He summed up the number of miles he had travelled for the reform of prisons, on his return to England after his journey, and another re-examination of the prisons at home, and found that the total was 42,033. Glorious *perseverance*! But he is away again! having found a new object for the yearnings of his ever-expanding heart. He conceived, from inquiries of his medical friends, that that most dreadful scourge of man's race—the plague—could be arrested in its destructive course. He visits Holland, France, Italy, Malta, Zante, the Levant, Turkey, Venice, Austria, Germany, and returns also by Holland to England. The narrative glows with interest in this tour; but the young reader—and how can he resist it if he have a heart to love what is most deserving of love—must turn to one of the larger biographies of Howard for the circumstances. Alas! a stroke was prepared for him on his return. His son, his darling son, had become disobedient, progressed fearfully in vice, and his father found him a raving maniac!

Howard's only refuge from this poignant affliction was in the renewal of the great mission of his life. He again visited the prisons of Ireland and Scotland, and left England to renew his humane course abroad, but never to return. From Amsterdam this tour extended to Cherson, in Russian Tartary.

Attending one afflicted with the plague there, he fell ill, and in a few days breathed his last. He wished to be buried where he died, and without pomp or monument: "Lay me quietly in the earth," said he; "place a sun-dial over my grave, and let me be forgotten!" Who would not desire at death that he had forgone every evanescent pleasure a life of selfishness could bring, to live and die like John Howard?

CONCLUSION.

Work, and the true nobility of being devoted to it, distinguished every exemplar recorded in our sketch; and no name of eminence or excellence can be selected in human annals who has ever used the phrase, which can only console idiots, that "he is perfectly happy, for he has nothing to do, and nothing to think about!" "Nothing to do!" in a world whose elements are, as yet, but partially subdued by man, and whose happiness can be augmented so incalculably by the perfecting of his dominion over Nature. "Nothing to think about!" when language, and poetry, and art, and music, and science, and invention, afford ecstatic occupation for thought which could not be exhausted if a man's life were even extended on the earth to a million of years. "Nothing to do, and nothing to think about!" while millions are doing and thinking,—for a human creature to profess that he derives pleasure from such a state of consciousness, is to confess his willingness to be fed, clothed, and attended by others, while he is meanly and despicably indolent and degradingly dependent.

Young reader, spurn the indulgence of a thought so unworthy of a human being! Remember, that happiness, worth the name, can never be gained unless in the discharge of duty, or under the sense of duty done. And work is duty—thy duty—the duty of all mankind. Whatever may be a man's situation, from the lowliest to the highest he has a work to perform as a bounden duty. Such was glorious Alfred's conviction as a king: such was Lackington's conviction as a tradesman. For every diversity of mind and genius the universe in which we live affords work, and the peculiar work for which each mind is filled becomes its bounden duty by natural laws. "First of all we ought to do *our own duty*—but, first of all," were the memorable death-bed words of Canova; and the conviction they expressed constituted the soul-spring of every illustrious man's life. The life of Canova was—work: so was the life of Shakspere, of Milton, of Jones, of Johnson, of Handel, of Davy, of Watt, of Newton, of all-glorious Howard. Their lives were "Triumphs of Perseverance:" even their deaths did not lessen their triumphs. "Being dead, they yet speak." They are ever present with us in their great words and thoughts, and in their great acts. Their spirits thus still conjoin to purify and enlighten the world: they are still transforming it, in some senses more effectually than if still living, from ignorance, and vice, and wrong and suffering, into a maturing sphere of knowledge and might over Nature, and justice and brotherhood. Let every earnest heart and mind be resolved on treading in their footsteps, and aiding in the realisation of the cheering trust that the world shall yet be a universally happy world, and so man reach that perfect consummation of the "TRIUMPHS OF PERSEVERANCE!"

THE
TRIUMPHS OF ENTERPRISE.

INTRODUCTION.

Without Enterprise there would have been no civilization, and there would now be no progress. To try, to attempt, to pass beyond an obstacle, marks the civilized man as distinguished from the savage. The advantage of passing beyond a difficulty by a single act of trial has offered itself, in innumerable instances, to the savage, but in vain; it has passed him by unobserved, unheeded. Nay, more: when led by the civilized man to partake of the advantages of higher life, the savage has repeatedly returned to his degradation. Thus it has often been with the native Australian. A governor of the colony, about sixty years ago, by an innocent stratagem took one of the native warriors into his possession, and strove to reconcile him to the habits of civilized life. Good clothes and the best food were given him; he was treated with the utmost kindness, and, when brought to England, the attention of people of distinction was lavished upon him. The Australian, however, was at length relanded in his own country, when he threw away his clothes as burdensome restraints upon his limbs, displayed his ancient appetite for raw meat, and in all respects became as rude as if he had never left his native wilderness. Another trial was made by a humane person, who procured two infants—a boy and a girl—believing that such an early beginning promised sure success. These young Australians were most carefully trained, fed, and clothed, after the modes of civilized Europe, and inured to the customs of our most improved society. At twelve years old they were allowed to choose their future life, when they rejected without hesitation the enjoyments of education, and fled to their people in the background to share their famine, nakedness, and cold.

A savage would perish in despair where the civilized man would readily discover the mode of extricating himself from difficulty; and yet, in point of physical strength, it might be that the savage was superior. Enterprise is thus clearly placed before the young reader as a quality of mind. He may display it without being gifted with strong corporeal power; it depends on thought, reflection, calculation of advantage. Whoever displays it is sure to be in some degree regarded with attention by his fellow men; it wins a man the way to public notice, and often to high reward, almost unfailingly. But the purpose of the ensuing pages is not to place false motives before the mind; to display any excellence with a view expressly to notice and reward and not from the wish to do good or to perform a duty, is unworthy of the truly correct man. The promptings of duty and beneficence are evermore to be kept before the mind as the only true guides to action.

In the instances of Enterprise presented in this little volume, the young reader will not discover beneficence to have been the invariable stimulant to action. Where the actor displays a deficiency in the high quality of mercy, the reader is recommended to think and judge for himself. The instances have been selected for their striking character, and the reader must class them justly. Let him call courage by its right name; and when it is not united with tenderness, let the act be weighed and named at its true value.

CHAPTER I.

The word "Enterprise," which, it has just been observed, marks the character of the civilized man as distinguished from the savage, might also be used with some degree of strictness to characterise man as distinguished from the lower animals. Their instincts enable some of them, as the bee and the beaver, to perform works of wondrous ingenuity; but none of them step beyond what has been the vocation of their species since it existed. The bounds of human exertion, on the other hand, are apparently illimitable. Its achievements in one generation, though deemed wonderful, are outstripped in the next; and the latest successful efforts of courage and skill serve to give us confidence that much or all which yet baffles man's sagacity and power in the realm of nature shall be eventually subjected to him; he is a being of Enterprise.

If endowed simply with bounded instincts he might have remained the wild inhabitant of the forest covert, or continued the rude tenant of the savage hut; his limitless, or, at least, indefinite and ever-progressing mental capacity, has empowered him to overcome obstacle after obstacle in the way to his increasing command over Nature; the triumphs of one generation have been handed down to the next, and the aggregate to those ages succeeding; and the catalogue of these "Triumphs of Enterprise" would now form a library of incalculable extent, since it would lead reflection into every path of the dominions of history and natural philosophy, of science and art.

The rudest display of this great characteristic of man is the assertion of his superiority to the rest of the animal world, and seems to offer a primary claim to observation. The stronger and fiercer animals would be the first enemies with which man had to struggle. With his conquest of their strength and ferocity, and subjection of some of their tribes to his use and service, his empire must have begun. Had we authentic records remaining of the earliest human essays towards taming the dog, domesticating the cat, and training for beneficial use or service the goat, the sheep, and the ox, the horse and the elephant, the camel, the llama, and the reindeer, such a chronicle would be filled with interest. Fable, however, surrounds the scanty memorials that remain of this as well as of higher departments of human discovery in the primeval ages. Abundant material exists in ancient history for a narrative of the more exciting part of these triumphs—the successful display of man's courage as opposed to the mightier strength of the more ferocious animals; but the accounts of such adventures in later times are less doubtful, and a brief recapitulation of a few of them will serve equally well to introduce the "Triumphs of Enterprise."

GENERAL PUTNAM,

Who signalised his courage in the struggles with the French on the continent of North America about the middle of the last century, removed after the war to the State of Connecticut. The wolves, then very numerous, broke into his sheepfold, and killed seven fine sheep and goats, besides wounding many lambs and kids. The chief havoc was committed by a she-wolf, which, with her annual litter of whelps, had infested the neighbourhood. The young were generally destroyed by the vigilance of the hunters, but the mother-wolf was too wary to come within gun-shot, and upon being closely pursued would fly to the western woods, and return the next winter with another litter of whelps. This wolf at length became such an intolerable nuisance that Putnam entered into a combination with five of his neighbours to hunt alternately until they could destroy her; two, by rotation, were to be constantly in pursuit. It was known that having lost the toes of one foot by a steel trap she made one track shorter than the other. By this peculiarity the pursuers recognised in a light snow the route of this destructive animal. Having followed her to Connecticut river and found that she had turned back in a direct course towards Pomfret, they immediately returned, and by ten o'clock the next morning the bloodhounds had driven her into a den about three miles from Putnam's house. The people soon collected with dogs, guns, straw, fire, and sulphur, to attack the common enemy. With these materials several unsuccessful efforts were made to force her from her den; the dogs came back badly wounded, and refused to return to the charge; the smoke of blazing straw had no effect, nor did the fumes of burnt brimstone, with which the cavern was filled, compel the wolf to quit her retirement. Wearied with such fruitless attempts, which had been continued until ten o'clock at night, Putnam tried once more to make his dog enter, but in vain. He proposed to his negro to go down into the cavern and shoot the wolf, but the negro dared not. Then it was that Putnam, declaring he would not have a coward in his family, and angry at the disappointment, resolved himself to destroy the ferocious beast or to perish in the attempt. His neighbours strongly remonstrated against the perilous undertaking; but he, knowing that wild animals are intimidated by fire, and having provided several slips of birch bark, the only combustible material which he could obtain that would afford light in this deep and darksome cave, prepared for his descent. Having divested himself of his coat and waistcoat, and fixed a strong rope round his body by which he might at a concerted signal be drawn out of the cave, he fearlessly entered head-foremost with the blazing torch in his hand.

The aperture of the den, on the east side of a very high ledge of rocks, was about two feet square; thence it descended obliquely fifteen feet, then running horizontally about ten more it ascended gradually sixteen feet towards its termination. The sides of this subterranean cavity were composed of smooth and solid rocks, which seem to have been driven from each other by some great convulsion of nature. The top and bottom were of stone, and the entrance to it in winter being covered with ice was exceedingly slippery. The cave was difficult of access, being in no place high enough for a man to stand upright, nor in any part more than three feet wide.

Having groped his passage to the horizontal part of the den, the most terrifying darkness appeared in front of the dim circle of light afforded by his torch. "It was silent as the tomb; none but monsters of the desert had ever before explored this solitary mansion of horror," says the relator. Putnam cautiously proceeded onward; came to the ascent, which he mounted on his hands and knees, and then discovered the glaring eyeballs of the wolf, which was sitting at the extremity of the cavern. Startled at the sight of the fire, she gnashed her teeth and gave a sullen growl. As soon as he had made the discovery he gave the signal for pulling him out of the cavern. The people at the mouth of the den, who had listened with painful anxiety, hearing the growling of the wolf, and supposing their friend to be in danger, drew him forth with such quickness that his shirt was stripped over his head and his body much lacerated. After he had adjusted his clothes and loaded his gun with nine buck shot, with a torch in one hand and his musket in the other, he descended a second time. He approached the wolf nearer than before. She assumed a still more fierce and terrible appearance, howling, rolling her eyes, and gnashing her teeth. At length, dropping her head between her legs, she prepared to spring upon him. At this critical moment he levelled his piece and shot her in the head. Stunned with the shock, and nearly suffocated with the smoke, he immediately found himself drawn out of the cave. Having refreshed himself and permitted the smoke to clear away, he entered the terrible cave a third time, when to his great satisfaction he found the wolf was dead; he then took hold of her ears, and making the necessary signal, the people above, with no small exultation, drew the wolf and her conqueror both out together.

From among the numerous records of successful encounter with tigers, let us select that of

LIEUT. EVAN DAVIES,

Which occurred while the British army was lying at Agoada, near Goa, 1809. A report was one morning brought to the cantonment that a very large tiger had been seen on the rocks near the sea. About nine o'clock a number of horses and men assembled at the spot where it was said to have been seen, when, after some search, the animal was discovered to be in the recess of an immense rock; dogs were sent in in the hope of starting him, but without effect, having returned with several wounds. Finding it impossible to dislodge the animal by such means, Lieut. Davies, of the 7th regiment, attempted to enter the den, but was obliged to return, finding the passage extremely narrow and dark. He attempted it, however, a second time, with a pick-axe in his hand, with which he removed some obstructions that were in the way. Having proceeded a few yards he heard a noise which he conceived to be that of the animal. He then returned, and communicated with Lieut. Threw, of the Artillery, who also went in the same distance, and was of a similar opinion. What course to pursue was doubtful. Some proposed to blow up the rock; others, to smoke the animal out. At length a port-fire was tied to the end of a bamboo, and introduced into a small crevice which led towards the den. Lieut. Davies went on hands and knees down the narrow passage which led to it, and by the light of his torch he was enabled to discover the animal. Having returned, he said he could kill him with a pistol, which, being procured, he again entered the cave and fired, but without success, owing to the awkward situation in which he was placed, having only his left hand at liberty. He next went with a musket and bayonet, and wounded the tiger in the loins; but he was obliged to retreat as quickly as the narrow passage would allow, the tiger having rushed forward and forced the musket back towards the mouth of the den. Lieut. Davies next procured a rifle, with which he again forced his way into the cave, and taking deliberate aim at the tiger's head, fired, and put an end to its existence. He afterwards tied a strong rope round the neck of the tiger, by which it was dragged out, to the no small satisfaction of a numerous crowd of spectators. The animal measured seven feet in length.

Combats with wild elephants are still more dangerous than with the tiger. From the following account given by a sojourner in India, the extreme hazard attending such enterprises will be seen, while a reflection can scarcely fail to arise on the wondrous superiority of man's sagacity which has enabled him to reduce this mightiest of land animals to docile servitude.

"We had intelligence," says the narrator, "of an immense wild elephant being in a large grass swamp within five miles of us. He had inhabited the swamp for years, and was the terror of the surrounding villagers, many of whom he had killed. He had only one tusk; and there was not a village for many miles round that did not know the 'Burrah ek durt ke Hathee,' or the large one-toothed elephant; and one of our party had the year before been charged and his elephant put to the right-about by this famous fellow. We determined to go in pursuit of him; and accordingly on the third day after our arrival, started in the morning, mustering, between private and government elephants, thirty-two, but seven of them only with sportsmen on their backs. As we knew that in the event of the wild one charging he would probably turn against the male elephants, the drivers of two or three of the largest were armed with spears. On our way to the swamp we shot a great number of different sorts of game that got up before the line of elephants, and had hardly entered the swamp when, in consequence of one of the party firing at a partridge, we saw the great object of our expedition. The wild elephant got up out of some long grass about two hundred and fifty yards before us, when he stood staring at us and flapping his huge ears. We immediately made a line of the elephants with the sportsmen in the centre, and went straight up to him until within a hundred and thirty yards, when, fearing he was going to turn from us, all the party gave him a volley, some of us firing two, three, and four barrels. He then turned round, and made for the middle of the swamp. The chase now commenced, and after following him upwards of a mile, with our elephants up to their bellies in mud, we succeeded in turning him to the edge of the swamp, where he allowed us to get within eighty yards of him, when we gave him another volley in his full front, on which he made a grand charge at us, but fortunately only grazed one of the pad elephants. He then made again for the middle of the swamp, throwing up blood and water from his trunk, and making a terrible noise, which clearly showed that he had been severely wounded. We followed him, and were obliged to swim our elephants through a piece of deep stagnant water, occasionally giving shot, when making a stop in some very high grass he allowed us again to come within sixty yards, and got another volley, on which he made a second charge more furious than the first, but was prevented making it good by some shots fired when very close to us, which stunned and fortunately turned him. He then made for the edge of the swamp, again swimming a piece of water, through which we followed with considerable difficulty in consequence of our pads and howdahs having become much heavier from the soaking they had got twice before. We were up to the middle in the howdahs, and one of the elephants fairly turned over and threw the rider and his guns into the water. He was taken off by one of the pad elephants, but his three guns went to the bottom. This accident took up some time, during which the wild elephant had made his way to the edge of the swamp, and stood perfectly still looking at us and trumpeting with his trunk. As soon as we got all to rights we again advanced with the elephants in the form of a crescent, in the full expectation of a desperate charge, nor were we mistaken. The animal now allowed us to come within forty yards of him, when we took a very deliberate aim at his head, and, on receiving this fire, he made a most furious charge, in the act of which, and when within ten yards of some of us, he received his mortal wound and fell dead as a stone. His death-wound on examination proved to be from a small ball over the left eye, for this was the only one of thirty-one that he had received in his head, which was found to have entered the brain. When down he measured in height twelve feet four inches; in length, from the root of the tail to the top of the head, sixteen feet; and ten feet round the neck. He had upwards of eighty balls in his head and body. His only remaining tusk when taken out weighed thirty-six pounds, and, when compared with the tusks of tame elephants, was considered small for the size of the animal. After he fell a number of villagers came about us, and were rejoiced at the death of their formidable enemy, and assured us that during the last four or five years he had killed nearly fifty men; indeed, the knowledge of the mischief he had occasioned was the only thing which could reconcile us to the death of so noble an animal."

Exciting as such accounts of contest with powerful land animals are, they yield in depth of interest to the records of the whale fishery. The potent combination of human courage and intelligence is so fully manifested by an excellent description of these daring but well ordered enterprises, contained in one of the volumes of the Edinburgh Cabinet Library, that we present it to the young reader almost entire:—

"As soon as they have arrived in those seas which are the haunt of the whale, the crew must be every moment on the alert, keeping watch day and night. The seven boats are kept hanging by the sides of the ship ready to be launched in a few minutes, and, where the state of the sea admits, one of them is usually manned and afloat. These boats are from twenty-five to twenty-eight feet long, about five and a half feet broad, and constructed with a special view to lightness, buoyancy, and easy steerage. The captain or some principal officer seated above surveys the water to a great distance, and the instant he sees the back of the huge animal which they seek to attack emerging from the waves, gives notice to the watch who are stationed on deck, part of whom leap into a boat, which is instantly lowered down, and followed by a second if the fish be a large one. Each of the boats has a harpooner and one or two subordinate officers, and is provided with an immense quantity of rope coiled together and stowed in different quarters of it, the several parts being spliced together so as to form a continued line usually exceeding four thousand feet in length; to the end is attached the harpoon, an instrument formed not to pierce and kill the animal, but by entering and remaining fixed in the body to prevent its escape. One of the boats is now rowed towards the whale in the deepest silence, cautiously avoiding to give any alarm, of which he is very susceptible. Sometimes a circuitous route is adopted in order to attack him from behind. Having approached as near as is consistent with safety, the harpooner darts his instrument into the back of the monster. This is a critical moment, for when this mighty animal feels himself struck he often throws himself into violent convulsive movements, vibrating in the air his tremendous tail, one lash of which is sufficient to dash a boat in pieces. More commonly, however, he plunges with rapid flight into the depths of the sea or beneath the thickest fields and mountains of ice. While he is thus moving, at the rate usually of eight or ten miles an hour, the utmost diligence must be used that the line to which the harpoon is attached may run off smoothly and readily along with him; should it be entangled for a moment the strength of the whale is such that he would draw the boat and crew after him under the waves. The first boat ought to be quickly followed up by a second to supply more line when the first is run out, which often takes place in eight or ten minutes. When the crew of a boat see the line in danger of being all run off, they hold up one, two, or three oars, to intimate their pressing need of a supply; at the same time they turn the rope once or twice round a kind of post called the bollard, by which the motion of the line and the career of the animal are somewhat retarded. This, however, is a delicate operation, which brings the side of the boat down to the very edge of the water, and if the rope be drawn at all too tight may sink it altogether. While the line is rolling round the bollard the friction is so violent that the harpooner is enveloped in smoke, and water must be constantly poured on to prevent it catching fire. When, after all, no aid arrives, and the crew find that the line must run out, they have only one resource—they cut it, losing thereby not only the whale but the harpoon and all the ropes of the boat.

"When the whale is first struck and plunges into the waves, the boat's crew elevate a flag as a signal to the watch on deck, who give the alarm to those asleep below by stamping violently on the deck, and crying aloud, 'A fall! a fall!' On this notice they do not allow themselves time to dress, but rush out in their sleeping-shirts or drawers into an atmosphere the temperature of which is often below zero, carrying along with them their clothing in a bundle and trusting to make their toilette in the interval of manning and pushing off the boats. Such is the tumult at this moment that young mariners have been known to raise cries of fear, thinking the ship was going down."

The period during which a wounded whale remains under water is various, but is averaged by Mr. Scoresby at about half an hour. Then, pressed by the necessity of respiration, he appears above, often considerably distant from the spot where he was harpooned and in a state of great exhaustion, which the same ingenious writer ascribes to the severe pressure that he has endured when placed beneath a column of water seven hundred or eight hundred fathoms deep. All the boats have meantime been spreading themselves in various directions, that one at least may be within a *start*, as it is called, or about two hundred yards at the point of his rising, at which distance they can easily pierce him with one or two more harpoons before he again descends, as he usually does for a few minutes. On his reappearance a general attack is made with lances, which are struck as deep as possible to reach and penetrate the vital parts. Blood mixed with oil streams copiously from his wounds and from his blow-holes, dyeing the sea to a great distance, and sprinkling and sometimes drenching the boats and crews. The animal now becomes more and more exhausted, but at the approach of his death he often makes a convulsive and energetic struggle, rearing his tail high in the air, and whirling it with a noise which is heard at the distance of several miles. At length, quite overpowered and exhausted, he lays himself on his side or back and expires. The flag is then taken down, and three loud huzzas raised from the surrounding boats. No time is lost in piercing the tail with two holes, through which ropes are passed, which, being fastened to the boats, drag the fish to the vessel amid shouts of joy.

One reflection must arise in the mind of the young reader—if he have begun to reflect—on reading this brief description of whale fishery enterprise. Man's attack upon the whale is *not* an act of self-defence; is it, then, justifiable? We cannot go into the whole argument which would present itself when such an important question is asked. We leave the reader to grapple with the difficulty as a healthy exercise for his understanding, only reminding him that the conveniences of civilization in the degree hitherto reached would be immensely curtailed if Man were not allowed to sacrifice for his own use the lives of animals which, either by their gentle nature or the localities they occupy, are without the range of the noxious and dangerous class.

CHAPTER II.

Equally early with their contests with wild animals primeval men would have had to encounter peril, and to overcome difficulty in the fulfilment of the natural desire possessed by some of them to visit new regions of the earth. Even if the theory be true which is supported by hundreds of learned volumes, that man's first habitation was in the most agreeable and fertile portion of Asia, by the banks of the Tigris and Euphrates, the native characteristic of enterprise would impel some among the first men to go in quest of new homes or on journeys of exploration and adventure; and, as the human family increased, removal for the youthful branches would be absolutely necessary.

To these primal travellers the perils of unknown adventure and the pressure of want would most probably have proved excitements too absorbing to have permitted a chronicle of their experience, even had the art of writing then existed. But details of adventure as wild and strange, perhaps, as any encountered by those earliest travellers exist in the volumes of recent discoverers; and while glancing at these we may imagine to ourselves similar enterprises of our race in the thousands of years which are past and gone. Let it be observed, in passing, that the young reader will find no books more rich and varied in interest than those of intelligent travellers; and if our slight mention of a few of their names as partakers in the "Triumphs of Enterprise" should induce him to form a larger acquaintance with their narratives, it can scarcely fail to induce thoughts and resolves that will tend to his advantage.

The perils to be undergone in desert regions are not more forcibly described by any travellers than by Major Denham, Dr. Oudney, and Captain Clapperton, the celebrated African discoverers. "The sand-storm we had the misfortune to encounter in crossing the desert," says the former, "gave us a pretty correct idea of the dreaded effects of these hurricanes. The wind raised the fine sand with which the extensive desert was covered so as to fill the atmosphere and render the immense space before us impenetrable to the eye beyond a few yards. The sun and clouds were entirely obscured, and a suffocating and oppressive weight accompanied the flakes and masses of sand which, I had almost said, we had to penetrate at every step. At times we completely lost sight of the camels, though only a few yards before us. The horses hung their tongues out of their mouths, and refused to face the torrents of sand. A sheep that accompanied the kafila (the travelling train), the last of our stock, lay down on the road, and we were obliged to kill him and throw the carcass on a camel. A parching thirst oppressed us, which nothing alleviated. We had made but little way by three o'clock in the afternoon, when the wind got round to the eastward and refreshed us a little; with this change we moved on until about five, when we halted, protected in a measure by some hills. As we had but little wood our fare was confined to tea, and we hoped to find relief from our fatigues by a sound sleep. That, however, was denied us; the tent had been imprudently pitched, and was exposed to the east wind, which blew a hurricane during the night; the tent was blown down, and the whole detachment were employed a full hour in getting it up again. Our bedding and every thing within the tent was during that time completely buried by the constant driving of the sand. I was obliged three times during the night to get up for the purpose of strengthening the pegs; and when in the morning I awoke two hillocks of sand were formed on each side of my head some inches high."

Dr. Oudney, the partner of Denham and Clapperton, in their adventurous enterprise, affords details more frightful in character. "Strict orders had been given during a certain day of the journey," he informs us, "for the camels to keep close up, and for the Arabs not to straggle—the Tibboo Arabs having been seen on the look out. During the last two days," he continues, "we had passed on the average from sixty to eighty or ninety skeletons each day; but the numbers that lay about the wells of El-Hammar were countless; those of two women, whose perfect and regular teeth bespoke them young, were particularly shocking—their arms still remained clasped round each other as they had expired, although the flesh had long since perished by being exposed to the burning rays of the sun, and the blackened bones only were left; the nails of the fingers and some of the sinews of the hand also remained, and part of the tongue of one of them still appeared through the teeth. We had now passed six days of desert without the slightest appearance of vegetation, and a little branch was brought me here as a comfort and curiosity. A few roots of dry grass, blown by the winds towards the travellers, were eagerly seized on by the Arabs, with cries of joy, for their hungry camels. Soon after the sun had retired behind the hills to the west, we descended into a wadey, where about a dozen stunted bushes, not trees, of palm marked the spot where water was to be found. The wells were so choked up with sand, that several cart-loads of it were removed previous to finding sufficient water; and even then the animals could not drink till nearly ten at night."

Nor was it merely the horrors of the climate which these intrepid travellers had to encounter. Their visitation of various savage tribes drew them into the circle of barbarous quarrels. The peril incurred by Major Denham, while accompanying the Bornou warriors in their expedition against the Felatahs, is unsurpassed for interest in any book of travels. "My horse was badly wounded in the neck, just above the shoulder, and in the near hind leg," says the Major, describing what had befallen himself and steed in the encounter; "an arrow had struck me in the face as it passed, merely drawing the blood. If either of my horse's wounds had been from poisoned arrows I felt that nothing could save me [The tribe he accompanied had been worsted.] However, there was not much time for reflection; we instantly became a flying mass, and plunged, in the greatest disorder, into that wood we had but a few hours before moved through with order, and very different feelings. The spur had the effect of incapacitating my beast altogether, as the arrow, I found afterwards, had reached the shoulder-bone, and in passing over some rough ground he stumbled and fell. Almost before I was on my legs the Felatahs were upon me; I had, however, kept hold of the bridle, and, seizing a pistol from the holsters, I presented it at two of these ferocious savages, who were pressing me with their spears: they instantly went off; but another, who came on me more boldly, just as I was endeavouring to mount, received the contents somewhere in his left shoulder, and again I was enabled to place my foot in the stirrup. Re-mounted, I again pushed my retreat; I had not, however, proceeded many hundred yards when my horse came down again, with such violence as to throw me against a tree at a considerable distance; and, alarmed at the horses behind, he quickly got up and escaped, leaving me on foot and unarmed. A chief and his four followers were here butchered and stripped; their cries were dreadful, and even now the feelings of that moment are fresh in my memory; my hopes of life were too faint to deserve the name. I was almost instantly surrounded, and incapable of making the least resistance, as I was unarmed. I was as speedily stripped; and, whilst attempting first to save my shirt and then my trousers, I was thrown on the ground. My pursuers made several thrusts at me with their spears, that badly wounded my hands in two places, and slightly my body, just under my ribs, on the right side; indeed I saw nothing before me but the same cruel death I had seen unmercifully inflicted on the few who had fallen into the power of those who now had possession of me. My shirt was now absolutely torn off my back, and I was left perfectly naked.

"When my plunderers began to quarrel for the spoil, the idea of escape came like lightning across my mind, and, without a moment's hesitation or reflection, I crept under the belly of the horse nearest me, and started as fast as my legs could carry me for the thickest part of the wood. Two of the Felatahs followed, and I ran on to the eastward, knowing that our stragglers would be in that direction, but still almost as much afraid of friends as of foes. My pursuers gained on me, for the prickly underwood not only obstructed my passage but tore my flesh miserably; and the delight with which I saw a mountain-stream gliding along at the bottom of a deep ravine cannot be imagined. My strength had almost left me, and I seized the young branches issuing from the stump of a large tree which overhung the ravine, for the purpose of letting myself down into the water, as the sides were precipitous, when, under my hand, as the branch yielded to the weight of my body, a large *liffa*, the worst kind of serpent this country produces, rose from its coil, as if in the act of striking. I was horror-stricken, and deprived for a moment of all recollection; the branch slipped from my hand, and I tumbled headlong into the water beneath; this shock, however, revived me, and with three strokes of my arms I reached the opposite bank, which with difficulty I crawled up, and then, for the first time, felt myself safe from my pursuers.

"Scarcely had I audibly congratulated myself on my escape, when the forlorn and wretched situation in which I was, without even a rag to cover me, flashed with all its force upon my imagination. I was perfectly collected, though fully alive to all the danger to which my state exposed me, and had already began to plan my night's rest in the top of one of the tamarind trees, in order to escape the panthers, which, as I had seen, abounded in these woods, when the idea of the *liffas*, almost as numerous and equally to be dreaded, excited a shudder of despair.

"I now saw horsemen through the trees, still farther to the east, and determined on reaching them if possible, whether friends or enemies. They were friends. I hailed them with all my might; but the noise and confusion which prevailed, from the cries of those who were falling under the Felatah spears, the cheers of the Arabs rallying and their enemies pursuing, would have drowned all attempts to make myself heard, had not the sheikh's negro seen and known me at a distance. To this man I was indebted for my second escape: riding up to me, he assisted me to mount behind him, while the arrows whistled over our heads, and we then galloped off to the rear as fast as his wounded horse could carry us. After we had gone a mile or two, and the pursuit had cooled, I was covered with a bornouse; this was a most welcome relief, for the burning sun had already begun to blister my neck and back, and gave me the greatest pain; and had we not soon arrived at water I do not think it possible that I could have supported the thirst by which I was being consumed."

The exciting narrative of travel in the central regions of Africa the young reader may pursue in various volumes, from those describing the adventures of Leo Africanus, in 1513, to the narrative of the intrepid career of Mungo Park, in 1796. From the dangers of travel in the torrid zone the spirit of contrast would direct us to a glance at the perils of adventure in the arctic. Here a pile of books written by men of science await us; but, unfortunately, many of them, like the volumes of Maupertuis and Pallas, though rich in details of natural philosophy or natural history, possess little interest as narratives of adventure. Their authors had little or none of the true heroic spirit of the man of enterprise, who never courts ease when the way of danger is the real path to entire knowledge. The spirit of Dr. Edward Daniel Clarke marks more accurately the proper constitution of the traveller united with the tendencies of the man of science. He had resolved to attempt reaching the North Pole; but having arrived at Enontakis, in latitude 68 degrees, 30 min., 30 sec., N., he was seized with illness, and obliged to return to the south. He thus writes to his mother, from Enontakis:—

"We have found the cottage of a priest in this remote corner of the world, and have been snug with him a few days. Yesterday I launched a balloon, eighteen feet in height, which I had made to attract the natives. You may guess their astonishment when they saw it rise from the earth. Is it not famous to be here within the frigid zone, more than two degrees within the arctic, and nearer to the pole than the most northern shores of Iceland? For a long time darkness has been a stranger to us. The sun, as yet, passes not below the horizon, but he dips his crimson visage behind a mountain to the north. This mountain we ascended, and had the satisfaction to see him make his courtesy without setting. At midnight the priest of this place lights his pipe, during three weeks of the year, by means of a burning-glass, from the sun's rays."

Of all travellers in the northern regions, though not the most intellectual, the hardiest and most adventurous is Captain Cochrane. He had originally intended to devote himself to African discovery, conceiving himself competent for that arduous undertaking, by experience of the fatigues he had borne in laborious pedestrian journeys through France, Spain, and Portugal, and in Canada. "The plan I proposed to follow," says he, "was nearly that adopted by Mungo Park, in his first journey—intending to proceed alone, and requiring only to be furnished with the countenance of some constituent part of the government. With this protection, and such recommendation as it would procure me, I would have accompanied the caravans in some servile capacity, nor hesitated even to sell myself as a slave, if that miserable alternative were necessary, to accomplish the object I had in view. In going alone, I relied upon my own individual exertions and knowledge of man, unfettered by the frailties and misconduct of others. I was then, as now, convinced that many people travelling together for the purpose of exploring a barbarous country, have the less chance of succeeding; more especially when they go armed, and take with them presents of value. The appearance of numbers must naturally excite the natives to resistance, from motives of jealousy or fear; and the danger would be greatly increased by the hope of plunder."

The answer he received from the Admiralty being unfavourable, and thinking that a young commander was not likely to be employed in active service, he planned for himself a journey on foot round the globe, as nearly as it could be accomplished by land, intending to cross from northern Asia to America at Behring's Straits. Captain Cochrane did not realise his first intent, but he tracked the breadth of the entire continent of Asia to Kamtschatka. Hazards and dangers befel him frequently in this enterprise; but he pursued it undauntedly. His perils commenced when he had left St. Petersburg but a few days, and had not reached Novogorod.

"From Tosna my route was towards Linbane," says our adventurer, "at about the ninth milestone from which I sat down, to smoke a cigar or pipe, as fancy might dictate. I was suddenly seized from behind by two ruffians, whose visages were as much concealed as the oddness of their dress would permit. One of them, who held an iron bar in his hand, dragged me by the collar towards the forest, while the other, with a bayonetted musket, pushed me on in such a manner as to make me move with more than ordinary celerity; a boy, auxiliary to these vagabonds, was stationed on the roadside to keep a look-out. We had got some sixty or eighty paces into the thickest part of the forest, when I was desired to undress, and having stripped off my trousers and jacket, then my shirt, and finally my shoes and stockings, they proceeded to tie me to a tree. From this ceremony, and from the manner of it, I fully concluded that they intended to try the effect of a musket upon me, by firing at me as they would at a mark. I was, however, reserved for fresh scenes; the villains, with much *sang froid*, seated themselves at my feet, and rifled my knapsack and pockets, even cutting out the linings of the clothes in search of bank bills or some other valuable articles. They then compelled me to take at least a pound of black bread, and a glass of rum, poured from a small flask which had been suspended from my neck. Having appropriated my trousers, shirts, stockings, and shoes, as also my spectacles, watch, compass, thermometer, and small pocket sextant, with one hundred and sixty roubles (about seven pounds), they at length released me from the tree, and, at the point of a stiletto, made me swear that I would not inform against them— such, at least, I conjectured to be their meaning, though of their language I understood not a word. Having received my promise, I was again treated by them to bread and rum, and once more fastened to the tree, in which condition they finally abandoned me. Not long after, a boy who was passing heard my cries, and set me at liberty. With the remnant of my apparel, I rigged myself in Scotch Highland fashion, and resumed my route. I had still left me a blue jacket, a flannel waistcoat, and a spare one, which I tied round my waist in such a manner that it reached down to the knees; my empty knapsack was restored to its old place, and I trotted on with even a merry heart."

He comes up with a file of soldiers in the course of a few miles and is relieved with some food, but declines the offer of clothes. A carriage is also offered to convey him to the next military station. "But I soon discovered," he continues, "that riding was too cold, and therefore preferred walking, barefooted as I was; and on the following morning I reached Tschduvo, one hundred miles from St. Petersburg." At Novogorod he is further relieved by the governor, and accepts from him a shirt and trousers.

He reaches Moscow without a renewal of danger, and thence Vladimir and Pogost. In the latter town he cheerfully makes his bed in a style that shows he possessed the spirit of an adventurer in perfection. "Being too jaded to proceed farther," are his words, "I thought myself fortunate in being able to pass the night in a *cask*. Nor did I think this mode of passing the night a novel one. Often, very often, have I, in the fastnesses of Spain and Portugal, reposed in similar style." He even selects exposure to the open air for sleep when it is in his power to accept indulgence. "Arrived at Nishney Novogorod, the Baron Bode," says he, "received me kindly, placing me for board in his own house; while for lodging I preferred the open air of his garden: there, with my knapsack for a pillow, I passed the night more pleasantly than I should have done on a bed of down, which the baron pressed me most sincerely to accept." A man who thus hardened himself against indulgence could scarcely dread any of the hardships so inevitable in the hazardous course he had marked out for himself.

Accordingly, we find him exciting the wonder of the natives by his hardihood, in the very heart of Siberia. "At Irkutsk," is his own relation, "in the month of January, with forty degrees of Reaumur, I have gone about, late and early, either for exercise or amusement, to balls or dinners, yet did I never use any other kind of clothing than I do now in the streets of London. Thus my readers must not suppose my situation to have been so desperate. It is true, the natives felt surprised, and pitied my apparently forlorn and hopeless situation, not seeming to consider that, when the mind and body are in constant motion, the elements can have little effect upon the person. I feel confident that most of the miseries of human life are brought about by want of a solid education—of firm reliance on a bountiful and ever-attendant Providence—of a spirit of perseverance—of patience under fatigue and privations, and a resolute determination to hold to the point of duty, never to shrink while life retains a spark, or while 'a shot is in the locker,' as sailors say. Often, indeed, have I felt myself in difficult and trying circumstances, from cold, or hunger, or fatigue; but I may affirm, with gratitude, that I have never felt happier than even in the encountering of these difficulties." He remarks, soon afterwards, that he has never seen his constitution equalled; but the young reader will remember that the undaunted adventurer has strikingly shown us how this excellent constitution was preserved from injury by shunning effeminacy.

Yet our traveller's superlative constitution is severely tested when he reaches the country of the Yakuti, a tribe of Siberian Tartars. He crosses a mountain range, and halts, with the attendants he has now found the means to engage, for the night, at the foot of an elevation, somewhat sheltered from the cold north wind. "The first thing on my arrival," he relates, "was to unload the horses, loosen their saddles or pads, take the bridles out of their mouths, and tie them to a tree in such a manner that they could not eat. The Yakuti then with their axes proceeded to fell timber, while I and the Cossack, with our lopatkas or wooden spades, cleared away the snow, which was generally a couple of feet deep. We then spread branches of the pine tree, to fortify us from the damp or cold earth beneath us; a good fire was now soon made, and each bringing a leathern bag from the baggage furnished himself with a seat. We then put the kettle on the fire, and soon forgot the sufferings of the day. At times the weather was so cold that we were obliged to creep almost into the fire; and as I was much worse off than the rest of the party for warm clothing, I had recourse to every stratagem I could devise to keep my blood in circulation. It was barely possible to keep one side of the body from freezing, while the other might be said to be roasting. Upon the whole, I passed the night tolerably well, although I was obliged to get up five or six times to take a walk or run, for the benefit of my feet. The following day, at thirty miles, we again halted in the snow, when I made a horse-shoe fire, which I found had the effect of keeping every part of me alike warm, and I actually slept well without any other covering than my clothes thrown over me; whereas, before, I had only the consolation of knowing that if I was in a freezing state with one half of my body, the other was meanwhile roasting to make amends."

Captain Cochrane's constitution had so much of the power of adaptation to circumstances, that he was enabled to make a meal even with the savagest tribes. A deer had been shot, and the Yakuti began to eat it uncooked! "Of course," says he, "I had the most luxurious part presented to me, being the marrow of the fore-legs. I did not find it disagreeable, though eaten raw and warm from life; in a frozen state I should consider it a great delicacy. The animal was the size of a good calf, weighing about two hundred pounds. Such a quantity of meat may serve four or five good Yakuti for a single meal, with whom it is ever famine or feast, gluttony or starvation."

The captain's account of the feeding powers of the Yakuti surpasses, indeed, anything to be found in the narratives of travellers which are proverbial for wonder. "At Tabalak I had a pretty good specimen," he continues, "of the appetite of a child, whose age could not exceed five years. I had observed it crawling on the floor, and scraping up with its thumb the tallow-grease which fell from a lighted candle, and I inquired in surprise whether it proceeded from hunger or liking of the fat. I was told from neither, but simply from the habit in both Yakuti and Tungousi of eating wherever there is food, and never permitting anything that can be eaten to be lost. I gave the child a candle made of the most impure tallow, a second, and a third—and all were devoured with avidity. The steersman then gave him several pounds of sour frozen butter; this also he immediately consumed. Lastly, a large piece of yellow soap—all went the same road; but as I was convinced that the child would continue to gorge as long as it could receive anything, I begged my companion to desist as I had done. As to the statement of what a man can or will eat, either as to quality or quantity, I am afraid it would be quite incredible. In fact, there is nothing in the way of fish or meat, from whatever animal, however putrid or unwholesome, but they will devour with impunity; and the quantity only varies from what they have to what they can get. I have repeatedly seen a Yakut or a Tungouse devour forty pounds of meat in a day. The effects are very observable upon them, for, from thin and meagre-looking men, they will become perfectly pot-bellied. I have seen three of these gluttons consume a reindeer at one meal."

These doings of the Siberian Tartars, our young readers will have rightly judged, however, are not among the most praiseworthy or dignified of the "Triumphs of Enterprise;" and we turn, with a sense of relief, to other scenes of adventure.

The grand mountain range of the Andes, or Cordilleras, with its rugged and barren peaks and volcanoes, and destitution of human habitants, sometimes for scores of miles in the traveller's route, has afforded a striking theme for many writers of their own adventures in South America. Mr. Temple, a traveller in 1825, affords us some exciting views of the perils of his journey from Peru to Buenos Ayres.

In the afternoon of one of these perilous days he had to ascend and descend the highest mountain he had ever yet crossed. After winding for more than two hours up its rugged side, and precisely in the most terrifying spot, the baggage-mule, which was in front, suddenly stopped. "And well it might, poor little wretch, after scrambling with its burden up such fatiguing flights of craggy steps!" exclaims this benevolent-minded traveller; "the narrowness of the path at this spot did not allow room to approach the animal to unload and give it rest. On one side was the solid rock, which drooped over our heads in a half-arch; on the other, a frightful abyss, of not less than two hundred feet perpendicular. Patience was, indeed, requisite here, but the apprehension was, that some traveller or courier might come in the contrary direction, and, as the sun was setting, the consequences could not fail of proving disastrous to either party. At one time, I held a council to deliberate on the prudence of freeing the passage by shooting the mule, and letting it roll, baggage and all, to the bottom. In this I was opposed by the postilion, though another as well as myself was of opinion that it was the only method of rescuing us from our critical situation before nightfall. I never felt so perplexed in my life. We were all useless, helpless, and knew not what to do. After upwards of half an hour—or, apprehension might add a few minutes to this dubious and truly nervous pause—the mule, of its own accord, moved on slowly for about twenty yards, and stopped again; then proceeded, then stopped; and thus, after two hours' further ascent, we gradually reached the summit. Two or three times I wished, for safety's sake, to alight, but actually I had not room to do so upon the narrow edge of the tremendous precipice on my left."

He was less fortunate in his return over the mountains of Tarija. "Cruel was the sight," says he, "to see us toiling up full fifteen miles continued steep to the summit of the Cordillera, that here forms a ridge round the south-western extremity of the province of Tarija; but crueller by far to behold the wretched, wretched mule, that slipped on the edge of the precipice, and—away! exhibiting ten thousand summersaults, round, round, round! down, down, down! nine hundred and ninety-nine thousand fathoms deep!—certainly not one yard less, according to the scale by which I measured the chasm in my wonder-struck imagination, while I stood in the stirrups straining forward over the ears of my horse (which trembled with alarm), and viewed the microscopic diminution of the mule, as it revolved with accelerated motion to the bottom, carrying with it our whole grand store of provision."

Here they were obliged to leave the poor animal to its fate, which there was no doubt would be that of being devoured by condors. But a far more serious accident befel Mr. Temple a few days after this. A favourite horse that he had purchased on his journey to Potosi got loose, and galloping off after a herd of his own species speedily disappeared, and was never recovered. His apostrophe to this animal is a specimen of fine benevolent sentiment. "My horse," said I to myself, "my best horse, my favourite horse, my companion, my friend, for so long a time, on journeys of so many hundred miles, carrying me up and down mountains, along the edge of precipices, across rivers and torrents, where the safety of the rider so often depended solely on the worthiness of the animal—to lose thee now in a moment of so much need, in a manner so unexpected, and so provokingly accidental, aggravated my loss. The constant care I took of thee proves the value I set on thy merits. At the end of many a wearisome journey, accommodation and comfort for thee were invariably my first consideration, let mine be what they might. Not even the severity of the past night could induce me to deprive thee of thy rug for my own gratification. And must I now suddenly say farewell? Then farewell, my trusty friend! A thousand dollars are in that portmanteau: had I lost every one of them, they must, indeed, have occasioned regret; but never could they have excited such a feeling of sorrow as thou hast, my best, my favourite horse—farewell!"

If we wished to depicture the earth as it must have appeared to primeval travellers, Humboldt, the most sagacious of adventurers, seems to assure us that South America approaches nearest to such a picture. "In this part of the new continent," he remarks, "surrounded by dense forests of boundless extent, we almost accustomed ourselves to regard men as not being essential to the order of nature. The earth is loaded with plants, and nothing impedes their free development. An immense layer of mould manifests the uninterrupted action of organic powers. The crocodiles and the boas are masters of the river; the jaguar, the pecari, the dante, and the monkeys traverse the forest without fear and without danger: there they dwell as in an ancient inheritance. This aspect of animated nature, in which man is nothing, has something in it strange and sad. To this we reconcile ourselves with difficulty on the ocean and amid the sands of Africa, though in these scenes, where nothing recals to mind our fields, our woods, and our streams, we are less astonished at the vast solitude through which we pass. Here, in a fertile country, adorned with eternal verdure, we seek in vain the traces of the power of man; we seem to be transported into a world different from that which gave us birth."

Of the suffering to be encountered by adventurers in these regions, we are assured, however, by Humboldt, the chief source does not consist in the presence of crocodiles or serpents, jaguars or monkeys. The dread of these sinks into nothing when compared to the *plaga de la moscas*—the torment of insects. "However accustomed," says Humboldt, "you may be to endure pain without complaint—however lively an interest you may take in the object of your researches—it is impossible not to be constantly disturbed by the musquetoes, zaucudoes, jejeus, and tempraneroes that cover the face and hands, pierce the clothes with their long sucker in the shape of a needle, and getting into the mouth and nostrils set you coughing and sneezing whenever you attempt to speak in the open air. I doubt whether there be a country on earth where man is exposed to more cruel torments in the rainy seasons, when the lower strata of the air to the height of fifteen or twenty feet are filled with venomous insects like a condensed vapour."

This terrific account of the American mosquito is confirmed by Mr. Hood, one of the companions of Captain Franklin, in the intrepid attempt to reach the North Pole by overland journey. "We had sometimes procured a little rest," he observes, "by closing the tent and burning wood or flashing gunpowder within, the smoke driving the musquitoes into the crannies of the ground. But this remedy was now ineffectual, though we employed it so perseveringly as to hazard suffocation. They swarmed under our blankets, goring us with their envenomed trunks and steeping our clothes in blood. We rose at daylight in a fever, and our misery was unmitigated during our whole stay. The food of the mosquito is blood, which it can extract by penetrating the hide of a buffalo; and if it is not disturbed it gorges itself so as to swell its body into a transparent globe. The wound does not swell, like that of the African mosquito, but it is infinitely more painful; and when multiplied an hundred-fold, and continued for so many successive days, it becomes an evil of such magnitude that cold, famine, and every other concomitant of an inhospitable climate, must yield pre-eminence to it. It chases the buffalo to the plains, irritating him to madness; and the reindeer to the sea-shore, from which they do not return till the scourge has ceased."

Captain Back, whose Arctic Land Expedition has made his name memorable, confirms these accounts. After describing the difficulties of himself and party in dragging their baggage and provisions, and even their canoe, up high, steep, and rugged ridges, over swamps of thick stunted firs, and open spaces barren and desolate, on which "crag was piled on crag to the height of two thousand feet from the base," he adds these descriptive sentences of the insect plague: "The laborious duty which had been thus performed was rendered doubly severe by the combined attack of myriads of sandflies and mosquitoes, which made our faces stream with blood. There is certainly no form of wretchedness among those to which the chequered life of a traveller is exposed, at once so great and so humiliating, as the torture inflicted by these puny blood-suckers. To avoid them is impossible; and as for defending himself, though for a time he may go on crushing by thousands, he cannot long maintain the unequal conflict, so that at last, subdued by pain and fatigue, he throws himself in despair with his face to the earth, and, half suffocated in his blanket, groans away a few hours of sleepless rest."

The swarms of sandflies, called *brulots* by the Canadians, it appears by the following account of Captain Back, are as annoying as the mosquitoes:—"As we dived into the confined and suffocating chasms, or waded through the close swamps, they rose in clouds, actually darkening the air. To see or speak was equally difficult, for they rushed at every undefended part and fixed their poisonous fangs in an instant. Our faces streamed with blood as if leeches had been applied, and there was a burning and irritating pain, followed by immediate inflammation, and producing giddiness which almost drove us mad. Whenever we halted, which the nature of the country compelled us to do often, the men—even the Indians—threw themselves on their faces, and moaned with pain and agony. My arms being less encumbered I defended myself in some degree by waving a branch in each hand; but, even with this and the aid of a veil and stout leather gloves, I did not escape without severe punishment. For the time I thought the tiny plagues worse even than mosquitoes."

The ardour which can bear a man onward through difficulties and annoyances of this nature is admirable; but love is united with our admiration when Capt. Back gives the following testimony to the benevolence of Sir John Franklin:—

"It was the custom of Sir John Franklin never to kill a fly; and though teased by them beyond expression, especially when engaged in taking observations, he would quietly desist from his work and patiently blow the half-gorged intruders from his hands—'the world was wide enough for both.' This was jocosely remarked upon by Akaitcho and the four or five Indians who accompanied him. But the impression, it seems," continues Captain Back, "had sunk deep, for on Manfelly's seeing me fill my tent with smoke, and then throw open the front and beat the sides all round with leafy branches to drive out the stupified pests before I went to rest, he could not refrain from expressing his surprise that I should be so unlike 'the old chief,' who would not destroy so much as a single mosquito." So true it is that the real hero, he for whom danger has no terrors, has the kindest and gentlest nature!

CHAPTER III.

He who first committed himself to the perils of the great waters must have been peculiarly distinguished among men for his intrepidity. Modern adventure on the wide ocean, or in comparatively unknown seas, is not accompanied with that uncertainty and sense of utter desolation which must have filled the mind of early adventurers when driven out of sight of land by the tempest; but neither the discovery of the compass nor the many other aids to safety possessed by modern navigators free their enterprises from appalling dangers. The persevering courage of travellers evermore commands our admiration; but the voyager takes his life in his hand from the moment that he leaves the shore. The freedom from fear—nay, the cheerfulness and exultation he experiences when surrounded by the waste of waters, far away from the enjoyments of house and home; the unsubduable resolution with which he careers over the wave and encounters every vicissitude of season and climate; the strength and vastness of the element itself which is the chief scene of his daring enterprise: these are considerations that ever interweave themselves with our ideal of the sea-adventurer, and render him the object of more profound and ardent admiration than the mere traveller by land.

To ourselves, as natives of a country whose greatness is owing to commercial enterprise and superiority in the arts of navigation, these remarks forcibly apply. Maritime discovery has been oftener, much oftener, undertaken by England and Englishmen than by any other country or people in the world. Many secondary reasons for this might be alleged in addition to the primary one of discovery. Such undertakings are the means of training our sailors to hardihood and young officers to the most difficult and dangerous situations in which a ship can be placed. They accustom the officers how to take care of and to preserve the health of a ship's company. They are the means of solid instruction in the higher branches of nautical science, and in the use of the various instruments which science has, of late years especially, brought to such perfection.

The career of the navigator thus assumes a higher character, being that of a pioneer of science and corroborator of its discoveries, than the employ or profession of any other man, however elevated the station allotted him by society. Reflection will convince the young reader that such men as Cook and Vancouver, Parry and Ross, are much more deserving of triumphal monuments than martial heroes. The dangers they encountered were fully as great, while the tendency of their grand enterprises was not to inflict suffering on mankind but to enlighten it with the knowledge of distant quarters of the globe, and to bless and enrich it by the improvement of navigation and commerce. For these reasons, the claim of the navigator to a high rank in our brief chronicle of the "Triumphs of Enterprise" would boldly assert itself, independent of the exciting nature of sea adventures.

Here is an hour of danger described by the heroic Ross, and occurring in the month of August, 1818, during that intrepid commander's search for the long wished-for "North-West Passage." "The two ships were caught by a gale of wind among the ice, and fell foul of each other. The ice-anchors and cables broke, one after another, and the sterns of the two ships came so violently into contact as to crush to pieces a boat that could not be removed in time. Neither the masters, the mates, nor those men who had been all their lives in the Greenland service, had ever experienced such imminent peril; and they declared that a common whaler must have been crushed to atoms. Our safety must, indeed, be attributed to the perfect and admirable manner in which the vessels had been strengthened when fitting for the service. But our troubles were not yet at an end; for, as the gale increased, the ice began to move with greater velocity, while the continued thick fall of snow kept from our sight the further danger that awaited us, till it became imminent. A large field of ice was soon discovered at a small distance, bearing fast down upon us from the west, and it thus became necessary to saw docks for refuge, in which service all hands were immediately employed. It was, however, found to be too thick for our nine-feet saws, and no progress could be made. This circumstance proved fortunate, for it was soon after perceived that the field, to which we were moored for this purpose, was drifting rapidly on a reef of icebergs which lay aground. The topsails were therefore close-reefed, in order that we might run, as a last resource, between two bergs, or into any creek that might be found among them; when suddenly the field acquired a circular motion, so that every exertion was now necessary for the purpose of warping along the edge, that being the sole chance we had of escaping the danger of being crushed on an iceberg. In a few minutes we observed that part of the field into which we had attempted to cut our docks, come in contact with the berg, with such rapidity and violence as to rise more than fifty feet up its precipitous side, where it suddenly broke, the elevated part falling back on the rest with a terrible crash, and overwhelming with its ruins the very spot we had previously chosen for our safety. Soon afterwards the ice appeared to us sufficiently open for us to pass the reef of bergs, and we once more found ourselves in a place of security."

The terrors of an iceberg scene are most graphically depicted by Ross, in the account of his second voyage of discovery. "It is unfortunate," says he, "that no description can convey an idea of a scene of this nature; and, as to pencil, it cannot represent motion or noise. And to those who have not seen a northern ocean in winter—who have not seen it, I should say, in a winter's storm—the term ice, exciting but the recollection of what they only know at rest, in an inland lake or canal, conveys no ideas of what it is the fate of an arctic navigator to witness and to feel. But let them remember that ice is stone; a floating rock in the stream, a promontory or an island when aground, not less solid than if it were a land of granite. Then let them imagine, if they can, these mountains of crystal hurled through a narrow strait by a rapid tide; meeting, as mountains in motion would meet, with the noise of thunder, breaking from each other's precipices huge fragments, or rending each other asunder, till, losing their former equilibrium, they fall over headlong, lifting the sea around in breakers, and whirling it in eddies; while the flatter fields of ice forced against these masses, or against the rocks, by the wind and the stream, rise out of the sea till they fall back on themselves, adding to the indescribable commotion and noise which attend these occurrences."

How tremendous must be the sense of danger to the tenants of a frail ship amidst such gigantic forces of nature, the most inexperienced reader can form some conception. But, overwhelming as the feeling of awe must be with the sailor surrounded with such terrors, it must be infinitely more tolerable than the prolonged and indescribably irksome heart-ache he experiences when inclosed for months in fixed ice, encompassed on every hand with desolation. "He must be a seaman," says the same gallant adventurer, "to feel that the vessel which bounds beneath him, which listens to and obeys the smallest movement of his hand, which seems to move but under his will, is 'a thing of life,' a mind conforming to his wishes: not an inert body, the sport of winds and waves. But what seaman could feel this as we did, when this creature, which used to carry us buoyantly over the ocean, had been during an entire year immoveable as the ice and the rocks around it, helpless, disobedient, dead? We were weary for want of occupation, for want of variety, for want of the means of mental exertion, for want of thought, and (why should I not say it?) for want of society. To-day was as yesterday—and as was to-day, so would be to-morrow: while, if there were no variety, no hope of better, is it wonderful that even the visits of barbarians were welcome? or can anything more strongly show the nature of our pleasures, than the confession that these visits were delightful—even as the society of London might be amid the business of London? When the winter has once in reality set in, our minds become made up on the subject; like the dormouse (though we may not sleep, which would be the most desirable condition by far), we wrap ourselves up in a sort of furry contentment, since better cannot be, and wait for the times to come: it was a far other thing to be ever awake, waiting to rise and become active, yet ever to find that all nature was still asleep, and that we had nothing more to do than to wish and groan, and—hope as we best might." How truly poetical his description of human feeling amidst the eternal appearance of ice and snow!—"When snow was our decks, snow was our awnings, snow our observations, snow our larders, snow our salt; and, when all the other uses of snow should be at last of no more avail, our coffins and our graves were to be graves and coffins of snow. Is this not more than enough of snow than suffices for admiration? Is it not worse, that during ten months in a year the ground is snow, and ice, and 'slush;' that during the whole year its tormenting, chilling, odious presence is ever before the eye? Who more than I has admired the glaciers of the extreme north? Who more has loved to contemplate the icebergs sailing from the Pole before the tide and the gale, floating along the ocean, through calm and through storm, like castles and towers and mountains, gorgeous in colouring, and magnificent, if often capricious, in form? And have I, too, not sought amid the crashing, and the splitting, and the thundering roarings of a sea of moving mountains, for the sublime, and felt that Nature could do no more? In all this there has been beauty, horror, danger, everything that could excite; they would have excited a poet even to the verge of madness. But to see, to have seen, ice and snow—to have felt snow and ice for ever, and nothing for ever but snow and ice, during all the months of a year—to have seen and felt but uninterrupted and unceasing ice and snow during all the months of four years—this it is that has made the sight of those most chilling and wearisome objects an evil which is still one in recollection, as if the remembrance would never cease."

To bid farewell to his ship in these regions of deathly solitariness must be a trial of the heart even severer than its sense of awe amid icebergs, or wearisomeness with the eternal snow. This fell to the lot of the brave Ross and his crew. Fast beset where there was no prospect of release, they commenced carrying forwards a certain quantity of provisions, and the boats with their sledges, for the purpose of advancing more easily afterwards. The labour of proceeding over ice and snow was most severe, and the wind and snow-drift rendered it almost intolerable. On the 21st of May, 1832 (for this was during Sir John Ross's *second* voyage) all the provisions from their ship, the Victory, had been carried forward to the several deposits, except as much as would serve for about a month. In the process of forming these deposits it was found that they had travelled, forwards and backwards, three hundred and twenty-nine miles to gain about thirty in a direct line. Preparation was now made for their final departure, which took place on the 29th of May.

"We had now," continues the commander, "secured everything on shore which could be of use to us in case of our return; or which, if we could not, would prove of use to the natives. The colours were therefore hoisted and nailed to the mast, we drank a parting glass to our poor ship, and having seen every man out, in the evening I took my own adieu of the Victory, which had deserved a better fate. It was the first vessel that I had ever been obliged to abandon, after having served in thirty-six, during a period of forty-two years.

It was like the last parting with an old friend; and I did not pass the point where she ceased to be visible without stopping to take a sketch of this melancholy desert—rendered more melancholy by the solitary, abandoned, helpless home of our past years, fixed in immovable ice till Time should perform on her his usual work."

After a full month's most fatiguing journey, they encamped and constructed a canvass-covered house. This they deserted, and set out once more, but, after several weeks' vain attempt to reach navigable water, were compelled to return, "their labours at an end, and themselves once more at home." Here—of the provisions left behind them—flour, sugar, soups, peas, vegetables, pickles, and lemon-juice, were in abundance; but of preserved meats there remained not more than would suffice for their voyage in the boats during the next season. A monotonous winter was spent in their house; and the want of exercise, of sufficient employment, short allowance of food, lowness of spirits produced by the unbroken sight of the dull, melancholy, uniform waste of snow and ice, had the effect of reducing the whole party to a more indifferent state of health than had hitherto been experienced.

"We were indeed all very weary of this miserable home," says Sir John Ross. "Even the storms were without variety: there was nothing to see out of doors, even when we could face the sky; and within it was to look equally for variety and employment and to find neither. If those of the least active minds dozed away their time in the waking stupefaction which such a state of things produces, they were the most fortunate of the party. Those among us who had the enviable talent of sleeping at all times, whether they were anxious or not, fared best."

At length the long-looked-for period arrived when it was deemed necessary to abandon the house in search of better fortune; and on the 7th of July, being Sunday, the last divine service was performed in their winter habitation. The following day they bid adieu to it for ever! and having been detained a short time at Batty Bay, and finding the ice to separate and a lane of water to open out, they succeeded in crossing over to the eastern side of Prince Regent Inlet. Standing along the southern shore of Barrow's Strait, on the 26th of August they discovered a sail, and, after some tantalizing delays, they succeeded in making themselves visible to the crew of one of her boats.

"She was soon alongside," proceeds Sir John Ross, "when the mate in command addressed us, by presuming that we had met with some misfortune and lost our ship. This being answered in the affirmative, I requested to know the name of his vessel, and expressed our wish to be taken on board. I was answered that it was the 'Isabella of Hull, once commanded by Captain Ross;' on which I stated that I was the identical man in question, and my people the crew of the Victory. That the mate who commanded this boat was as much astonished at this information as he appeared to be I do not doubt; while, with the usual blunderheadedness of men on such occasions, he assured me that I had been dead two years! I easily convinced him, however, that what ought to have been true, according to his estimate, was a somewhat premature conclusion, as the bear-like form of the whole set of us might have shown him had he taken time to consider that we were certainly not whaling gentlemen, and that we carried tolerable evidence of our being 'true men, and no impostors' on our backs, and in our starved and unshaven countenances. A hearty congratulation followed, of course, in the true seaman style, and after a few natural inquiries he added that the 'Isabella was commanded by Captain Humphreys,' when he immediately went off in his boat to communicate his information on board, repeating that we had long been given up as lost, not by them alone, but by all England.

"As we approached slowly after him to the ship, he jumped up the side, and in a minute the rigging was manned, while we were saluted with three cheers as we came within cable's length, and were not long in getting on board of my old vessel, where we were all received by Captain Humphreys with a hearty seaman's welcome.

"Though we had not been supported by our names and characters, we should not the less have claimed, from charity, the attentions that we received, for never was seen a more miserable-looking set of wretches; while, that we were but a repulsive-looking people, none of us could doubt. If to be poor, wretchedly poor, as far as all our present property was concerned, was to have a claim on charity, no one could well deserve it more; but if to look so as to frighten away the so-called charitable, no beggar that wanders in Ireland could have outdone us in exciting the repugnance of those who have not known what poverty can be. Unshaven since I know not when, dirty, dressed in the rags of wild beasts instead of the tatters of civilization, and starved to the very bones, our gaunt and grim looks, when contrasted with those of the well-dressed and well-fed men around us, made us all feel, I believe for the first time, what we really were as well as what we seemed to others. Poverty is without half its mark unless it be contrasted with wealth; and what we might have known to be true in the past days, we had forgotten to think of till we were thus reminded of what we truly were as well as seemed to be.

"But the ludicrous soon took place of all other feelings; in such a crowd and such confusion all serious thought was impossible, while the new buoyancy of our spirits made us abundantly willing to be amused by the scene which now opened. Every man was hungry and was to be fed, all were ragged and were to be clothed, there was not one to whom washing was not indispensable, nor one whom his beard did not deprive of all English semblance. All, everything, too, was to be done at once; it was washing, dressing, shaving, eating, all intermingled; it was all the materials of each jumbled together; while, in the midst of all, there were interminable questions to be asked and answered on all sides: the adventures of the Victory, our own escapes, the politics of England, and the news which was now four years old. But all subsided into peace at last. The sick were accommodated, the seamen disposed of, and all was done for all of us which care and kindness could perform. Night at length brought quiet and serious thoughts, and I trust there was not one man among us who did not then express, where it was due, his gratitude for that interposition which had raised us all from a despair which none could now forget, and had brought us from the very borders of a not distant grave to life, and friends, and civilization.

"Long accustomed, however, to a cold bed on the hard snow or the bare rock, few could sleep amid the comfort of our new accommodations. I was myself compelled to leave the bed which had been kindly assigned me and take my abode in a chair for the night, nor did it fare much better with the rest. It was for time to reconcile us to this sudden and violent change, to break through what had become habit, and to inure us once more to the usages of our former days."

As a curious contrast to these exciting descriptions of danger, we will sketch in as compact a form as possible the first voyage round the world performed by an Englishman—namely, our illustrious countryman, Sir Francis Drake.

Queen Elizabeth, on presenting a sword to the commander of a secret expedition, said, "We do account that he which striketh at thee, Drake, striketh at us." His fleet consisted of five ships—the Pelican, of 120 tons burthen; the Elizabeth, a bark of 80 tons; the Swan, a fly-boat of 50 tons; the Marygold, a barque of 30 tons, and the Christopher, a pinnace of 15 tons, and was ostensibly fitted out for a trading voyage to Alexandria, though this pretence did not deceive the watchful Spaniards. Drake, like Columbus and Cook, chose small ships as better fitted to thread narrow and difficult channels. The crews of his little squadron amounted to one hundred and sixty men; an old author says that he did not omit "provision for ornament and delight, carrying with him expert musicians, rich furniture (all the vessels for his table, yea, many belonging to his cook-room, being of pure silver), with divers shows of all sorts of curious workmanship whereby the civility and magnificence of his native country might, among all nations whither he should come, be the more admired."

Although it is likely that the intrepid resolve of crossing the Pacific Ocean was not originally formed by Drake, and only entered into from circumstances in which he was afterwards placed, he is not the less entitled to the praise so often given him for penetrating with so small a force the channel explored by Magellan and known by his name. The passage through the Straits of Magellan had long been abandoned by the Spaniards, and a superstition had arisen against adventuring into the Pacific, as likely to prove fatal to any who are engaged in the discovery or even in the navigation of its waters.

Drake was at first driven back by a violent storm; but, unintimidated by this adverse augury, he finally set sail from Plymouth on the 13th of December, 1577. On Christmas-day they reached Cape Cantin, on the coast of Barbary, and on the 27th found a safe and commodious harbour in Mogadore. Here Drake had some unpleasant transactions with Muley Moloc, the celebrated king of the Moors, but sailed again on the last day of the year. The less important places touched at in the succeeding part of the voyage were Cape Blanco, the isles of Mayo and San Jago, and the "Isla del Fogo," or Burning Island, together with "Ilba Brava," or the Brave Island. The equinoctial line is afterwards crossed amidst alternate calms and tempest; they are supplied with fresh water by copious rains, and they also catch dolphins, bonitos, and flying-fish which fell on the decks, "where hence," says the invaluable Hakluyt, "they could not rise againe for want of moisture, for when their wings are drie they cannot flie." At length, on the 5th of April, they had fully voyaged across the wide Atlantic, and made the coast of Brazil in 31° 30′ south latitude. They saw the natives raising fires on the shore, beheld troops of wild deer, "large and mightie," and saw the foot-prints of men of large stature on the beach. On the 15th of the same month they anchored in the great River Plate, where they killed "certaine sea-wolves, commonly called seales." They thus secured a new supply of fresh provisions, and shortly after of fresh water.

On the 27th they again stood out to sea, and steered southward. The Swan was outsailed by the rest of the little fleet, and also the Mary, a very small Portuguese vessel, or caunter, which they had taken in their course. On the 12th of May, Drake anchored within view of a headland, and the next morning went in a boat to the shore. Here he was in some danger, for a thick fog came on and shut him from the view of the vessels; a gale also arose and drove them out to sea. Fires were at length lighted, all the vessels, save the Swan and the Mary, were again collected together. Fifty dried ostriches, besides other fowls, are related to have been here found deposited by the savages, and of this store the ships' crews took possession. Upwards of two hundred seals were also taken and slaughtered; and while a party was filling water-casks, killing seals, and salting fowls for future provision, Drake himself set sail in the Pelican, and Captain Winter in the Elizabeth, each on different tacks, in search of the Swan and the Mary. Drake soon found the Swan, and, to diminish the cares and hazards of the voyage, removed all her stores and then broke her up for firewood.

The place of rendezvous was named Seal Bay, and some highly interesting accounts of interviews with the savage native tribes during their stay here are given in Hakluyt. On the 3rd of June they set sail once more; on the 19th they found the missing Portuguese prize, the Mary; and the next day the whole squadron moored in Port San Julian, latitude 49° 30′ S.

A very perilous squabble took place here with the native Patagonians. A gunner belonging to the crew was shot through with an arrow, and died on the spot, and Robert Winter, relative of the officer above mentioned, was wounded, and died in consequence shortly afterwards. The stature of these tribes has been the subject of dispute from the time of Magellan to our own. An old author in Hakluyt says, "These men be of no such stature as the Spaniardes report, being but of the height of Englishmen: for I have seene men in England taller than I could see any of them. But peradventure the Spaniard did not thinke that any Englishman would have come thither so soone to have disproved them in this and divers others of their notorious lies." Another author, however, makes the Patagonians seven feet and a half in height.

An event occurred while the fleet lay at Port San Julian, which has cast a deep shade of suspicion over the character of Drake. This was the execution of Thomas Doughty, accused of mutiny and a conspiracy to massacre Drake and the principal officers. We leave the young reader to investigate the matter in other works, and proceed with our abridged narrative.

After breaking up the Portuguese prize and reducing the number of ships to three, they again set sail on the 17th of August—the weather being colder than midwinter in Britain—and on the 24th anchored thirty leagues within the Strait of Magellan. Here Drake changed the name of his ship, the Pelican, to the Golden Hind, in compliment to his friend, Sir Christopher Hatton, in whose escutcheon the golden hind is said to have had a place. While passing through the strait, which they computed to be 110 leagues in length, they noted that the width varied from one league to four; that the tide set in from each end of the strait and met about the middle; and they also killed 3000 "of birds having no wings, but short pineons which serve their turne in swimming." These penguins, as they undoubtedly were, are also described as being "fat as an English goose."

On the 6th of September, 1578, Drake and his gallant crew sailed their ships on the great Pacific. Magellan had passed through the strait in 1520, and but two other voyagers had performed the passage after Magellan, and before Drake.

A north-east passage was one main object contemplated by Drake; and accordingly, on clearing the strait, he held a north-west course, and in two days the fleet advanced seventy leagues. A violent gale from the north-east now drove them into 57° south latitude and 200 leagues to the west. Under bare poles they scudded before the tempest, and observed an eclipse of the moon on the 15th of September; "but," says a narrator, in Hakluyt, "neyther did the eclipticall conflict of the moon impayre our state, nor her clearing againe amend us a whit, but the accustomed eclipse of the sea continued in his force, wee being darkened more than the moone sevenfold." After a short season of moderate weather, another tempest separated from them the ship Marygold, and she was never more heard of. The Golden Hind and Elizabeth were now left to pursue the voyage; but on being driven back to the western entrance of the strait, Winter, the commander of the Elizabeth, heartily tired of the voyage, slipped away from Drake and returned to England. He reached this country in June, 1579, with the credit of having achieved the navigation of the Straits of Magellan, but with the shame of having deserted his commander.

The gallant Drake in the Golden Hind had stormy weather to encounter for some time after, and was driven so far south as to anchor in a creek at Cape Horn, and thus became the discoverer of that southern point of the entire continent of America.

The wind changing he steered northwards, and on the 25th of November, 1578, anchored near the coast of Chili, where he had another collision with the natives and lost two of his men. Soon afterwards they fell in with a people of more friendly manners, and learned that they had oversailed Valparaiso, the port of San Jago, where a Spanish ship lay at anchor. They put back and took the ship, called the Grand Captain of the South, in which were 60,000 pesos of gold, besides jewels, merchandise, and a good store of Chili wine. Each peso was valued at eight shillings. They rejoiced over their plunder; but in our own times such an act would be deemed a piracy. Nine families inhabited Valparaiso, but they fled, and the English revelled in the pillage of wine, bread, bacon, and other luxuries to men long accustomed to hard fare.

They plundered the church also of a silver chalice, two cruets, and an altar-cloth, and presented them to the chaplain of the vessel.

On the 19th of January, 1579, after some period of rest in a harbour, they pursued their voyage along the coast, and accidentally landing at Tarapaza, they found a Spaniard asleep on the shore with thirteen bars of silver lying beside him. "We took the silver and left the man," says the relator. A little farther on a party which was sent ashore to procure water fell in with a Spaniard and a native boy driving eight llamas, each of which was laden with two leathern bags containing fifty pounds of silver, or eight hundred in all. They not only took on board the llamas and the silver, but soon after fell in with three small barks quite empty (the crews being on shore), save that they found in them fifty-seven wedges of silver, each weighing twenty pounds. They took the silver and set the barks adrift. After some other trifling adventures they learned that the Cacafuego, a ship laden with gold and silver, had just sailed for Panama, the point whence all goods were carried by the Spaniards across the isthmus. Away they bore in search of this ship, but were near being overtaken by a superior force of Spaniards in two ships. Escaping, they passed Payta, and learned that the Cacafuego had the start of them but two days. Two other vessels were next taken, with some silver, eighty pounds of gold, and a golden crucifix "with goodly great emerauds set in it." The Cacafuego was at length overtaken and captured: the ship contained twenty-six tons of silver, thirteen chests of rials of plate, and eighty pounds of gold, besides diamonds and inferior gems, the whole estimated at 360,000 pesos. The uncoined silver alone found in the vessel may be estimated at 212,000*l.*, at five shillings an ounce.

It seems questionable whether, when thus richly laden, Drake would have thought of encompassing the globe if he could have assured himself of a safe voyage to England by returning through the Straits of Magellan. He knew that the Spaniards would be on the alert to recover the treasure, and so resolved to seek a north-east passage homeward. After remaining a short time in a safe harbour to repair the ship, he commenced the voyage once more. Delays were made for plunder and prizetaking until the 26th of April, when Drake stood boldly out to sea, and by the 3rd of June had sailed 1400 leagues on different courses without seeing land. He had now reached 42° north latitude, and the cold was felt severely. On the 5th, being driven by a gale, land was seen, to the surprise of Drake, who had not calculated that the continent stretched so far westward. The adventurers were now coasting the western margin of California.

They anchored at length in 38° 30′ north latitude, and were soon surrounded with native Indians, who, among other remarkable things, offered them *tabah*, or tobacco. Drake spent thirty-six days here for completing the repairs of his ship, took possession of the country formally, by erecting a monument and fixing a brass plate upon it, bearing the name, effigy, and arms of Queen Elizabeth, and called the country New Albion. To the port in which they had anchored he gave his own name, and on the 23rd of July bore away direct west as possible across the Pacific, with the intent to reach England by India and the Cape of Good Hope.

No land was seen by the gallant men on board this little ship for sixty-eight days. On the 30th of September they fell in with some islands in 8° north latitude, which they termed the Isle of Thieves, from the dishonest disposition of the natives. On the 16th of October they reached the Philippines, and anchored at Mindanao. On the 3rd of November the Moluccas were seen, and they soon anchored before the chief town of Ternate, entered into civil gossip with the natives, and were visited by the king, "a true gentleman Pagan." Among the presents received from this royal person were fowls, rice, sugar, cloves, figs, and "a sort of meale which they call *sagu*, made of the tops of certaine trees, tasting in the mouth like soure curds, but melteth like sugar, whereof they make certaine cakes, which may be kept the space of ten yeeres and yet then good to be eaten." Brilliant offers were made by the Sultan of Ternate; but Drake was shy of them, and on the 9th of November, having taken in a large quantity of cloves, the Golden Hind left the Moluccas.

On the 14th they anchored near the eastern part of Celebes, and finding the land uninhabited and abundant in forests, they determined there fully to repair the ship for her voyage home. "Throughout the groves," say the old writers in Purchas and Hakluyt, "there flickered innumerable bats 'as bigge as large hennes.' There were also multitudes of 'fiery wormes flying in the ayre,' no larger than the common fly in England, which skimming up and down between woods and bushes, made "such a shew and light as if every twigge or tree had bene a burning candle." They likewise saw great numbers of land-crabs, or cray-fish, "of exceeding bignesse, one whereof was sufficient for foure hungry stomackes at a dinner, being also very good and restoring meat, whereof wee had experience; and they digge themselves holes in the earth like conies."

On the 12th of December they again set sail; but now came their great peril. After being entangled in shoals among the Spice Islands for some days, in the night of the 9th of January, 1580, the Golden Hind struck on a rock. No leak appeared; but the ship was immovable. The ebb tide left her in but six feet water, while, so deeply was she laden, that it required thirteen feet of water to float her. Eight guns, three tons of cloves, and a quantity of meal were thrown overboard, but this did not relieve the ship. "We stucke fast," says the narrator in Hakluyt, "from eight of the clocke at night til foure of the clocke in the afternoone the next day, being indeede out of all hope to escape the danger; but our generall, as he had always hitherto shewed himself couragious, and of a good confidence in the mercie and protection of God, so now he continued in the same; and lest he should seeme to perish wilfully, both hee and wee did our best indevour to save ourselves, which it pleased God so to blesse, that in the ende we cleared ourselves most happily of the danger."

Their ship in deep water once more, they reached the Isle of Barateve on the 8th of February, and were kindly and handsomely treated by the inhabitants. Java was reached on the 12th of March, and here again they were generously received. On the 26th they left Java, and did not again see land till they passed the Cape of Good Hope, on the 15th of June. The Portuguese being acquaintances, Drake did not wish just then to meet; he did not land at the Cape, but steered away north, and on the 22nd of July arrived at Sierra Leone. Finally, on the 26th of September, 1580, after an absence of two years and ten months, he came to anchor in the harbour of Plymouth.

The riches he had brought home, the daring bravery he had displayed, the perils undergone, the marvels told of the strange countries visited, made Drake the idol of the whole English people. On the 4th of April, 1581, Queen Elizabeth went in state to dine on board the Golden Hind, then lying at Deptford. After the banquet she knighted the gallant circumnavigator, and also gave orders that his vessel should be preserved as a monument of the glory of the nation and of the illustrious voyager.

CHAPTER IV.

One path of Enterprise belongs distinctly to modern adventurers—the search after interesting remains of antiquity, and investigation of their present actual condition. Such enterprises of discovery have often their source in a love of Art, which can only exist in the most cultivated minds. In other instances they arise from a laudable desire to verify ancient history, and thus serve the highly important purpose of confirming that branch of human knowledge which has hitherto depended simply on the testimony of written tradition.

Perhaps the greatest contributor to certain knowledge in this department of enterprise and discovery was the celebrated Belzoni, though our acquaintance with the time-honoured and mysterious monuments of Egypt has been enlarged by many other travellers. Greece has also had her distinguished list of antiquarian explorers; and the glowing lands of the East, so famous in sacred and profane story, have been visited by numerous travellers, each and all ardent to survey and report the present condition of the diversified monuments of human skill and strength existing in the primeval countries of our race.

Every youthful visitor to the British Museum will be interested with the beautiful black granite statue so well known as "the young Memnon." Near the left foot of this gigantic sitting figure will be found the name of Belzoni, cut by his own hand. Burckhardt and Salt were the enterprising and disinterested persons who paid the expenses of conveying this massive piece of ancient sculpture to Alexandria: Belzoni and his assistants undertook the immense labour.

The Ruins of Luxor.

It was amidst the ruins of Thebes, old Homer's "city of the hundred gates," that this far-famed statue of an old Egyptian king had long lain. His wonder at entering this ruined metropolis is thus described by Belzoni: "We saw for the first time the ruins of great Thebes, and landed at Luxor. Here I beg the reader to observe that but very imperfect ideas can be formed of the extensive ruins of Thebes, even from the accounts of the most skilful and accurate travellers. It is absolutely impossible to imagine the scene displayed without seeing it. The most sublime ideas that can be formed from the most magnificent specimens of our present architecture would give a very incorrect picture of these ruins; for such is the difference, not only in magnitude, but in form, proportion, and construction, that even the pencil can convey but a faint idea of the whole. It appeared to me like entering a city of giants, who, after a long conflict, were all destroyed, leaving the ruins of their various temples as the only proof of their former existence. The temple of Luxor presents to the traveller at once one of the most splendid groups of Egyptian grandeur. The extensive propylæon, with the two obelisks, and colossal statues in the front; the thick groups of enormous columns; the variety of apartments and the sanctuary it contains; the beautiful ornaments which adorn every part of the walls and columns, cause in the astonished traveller an oblivion of all that he has seen before. If his attention be attracted to the north side of Thebes by the towering remains that project a great height above the wood of palm trees, he will gradually enter that forest-like assemblage of ruins of temples, columns, obelisks, colossi, sphynxes, portals, and an endless number of other astonishing objects, that will convince him at once of the impossibility of a description. On the west side of the Nile, still the traveller finds himself among wonders. The temples of Gournou, Memnonium, and Medinet Aboo, attest the extent of the great city on this side. The unrivalled colossal figures in the plain of Thebes, the number of tombs excavated in the rocks, those in the great valley of the kings, with their paintings, sculptures, mummies, sarcophagi, figures, &c., are all objects worthy of the admiration of the traveller, who will not fail to wonder how a nation which was once so great as to erect these stupendous edifices could so far fall into oblivion that even their language and writing are totally unknown to us."

Ruins of the Temple of Memnon.

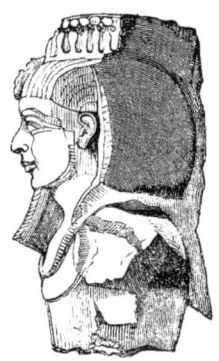

Bust of Memnon.

The bust of Memnon, the immediate object of Belzoni's research, soon caught his eye. It was lying with its face upwards, and "apparently smiling on me," says Belzoni, "at the thought of being taken to England." Among a semi-barbarous people like the Arabs the discoverer had a thousand difficulties to overcome before he could succeed in moving this bust of ten or twelve tons weight one inch from its bed of sand. The chiefs eyed him with jealousy, and conceived, as usual, that he came in quest of hidden treasures; and the Fellahs were with difficulty set to work, having made up their minds that it was a hopeless task. When these simple people saw it first move they all set up a loud shout, declaring it was not their exertions but the power of the devil that had effected it. The enormous mass was put in motion by a few poles and palm-leaf ropes, all the means which they could command, and which nothing but the ingenuity of Belzoni could have made efficient. But these materials, poor as they were, created not half the difficulty and delay occasioned by the intrigues of the Cachefs and Kaimakans, all of whom were desirous of extorting as much money as they possibly could, and of obstructing the progress of the work, as the surest means of effecting their purpose. Even the labourers, on finding that money was given to them for removing a mere mass of stone, took it into their heads that it must be filled with gold, and agreed that so precious an article ought not to be taken out of the country. Belzoni succeeded, however, in allaying these ridiculous imaginings, and eighteen days after the commencement of the operation the colossal bust reached the banks of the Nile. One day was consumed in embarking it; and after a voyage of hazard among the cataracts of the Nile, the illustrious traveller reached Cairo with his prize. From thence he conveyed it to Alexandria, and lodged it in the Pasha's magazine; he then returned to Cairo, and accompanied by Mr. Beechy, immediately proceeded up the Nile, with the determination, if possible, to accomplish the opening of the great temple of Ipsambul, a labour he had commenced but a short time before.

Belzoni Removing the Bust of Memnon.

This grand and gigantic relic of antiquity was discovered and brought into notice by the lamented Burckhardt, but when Belzoni first approached it, the accumulation of sand was such "that it appeared an impossibility ever to reach the door." The exact spot where he had fixed the entrance to be was determined in his own mind from observing the head of a hawk, of such a monstrous size that, with the body, it could not be less than twenty feet high. This bird he concluded to be over the doorway; and as below the figure there is generally a vacant space, followed by a frieze and cornice, he calculated the upper part of the doorway to be about thirty-five feet below the summit of the sand.

Having succeeded in procuring for hire, from one of the cachefs, as many labourers as he could afford to employ, Belzoni set about clearing away the sand from the front of the temple. The only condition made with the cachef was, that all the gold and jewels found in it should belong to him, as chief of the country, and that Belzoni should have all the stones. At the end of four or five days his funds were entirely exhausted; he therefore, after obtaining a promise from the chief that no one should molest the work in his absence, resumed his search for other antiquities; and, after conveying the Memnon to Alexandria, and being joined by Mr. Beechy at Cairo, met, at Philæ, with Captains Irby and Mangles of the British Navy, and was joined also by them.

Having conciliated the cachefs by suitable presents, they agreed to give the workmen, who were eighty in number, three hundred piastres for removing the sand as low down as the entrance. At first they seemed to set about the task like men who were determined to finish the job; but, at the end of the third day, they all grew tired, and, "under the pretext that the Rhamadan was to commence on the next day, they left us," says Belzoni, "with the temple, the sand, and the treasure, and contented themselves with keeping the three hundred piastres."

The travellers were now convinced that, if the temple was to be opened at all, it must be by their own exertions; and, accordingly assisted by the crew of the boat, they set to work, and, by dint of perseverance and hard labour for about eighteen days, they arrived at the doorway of that temple, which had, in all probability, been covered with sand two thousand years, and which proved to be the finest and most extensive in Nubia. Belzoni thus describes the exterior of the temple of Ipsambul.

"The outside of this temple is magnificent. It is a hundred and seventeen feet wide, and eighty-six feet high: the height from the top of the cornice to the top of the door being sixty-six feet six inches, and the height of the door twenty feet. There are four enormous sitting colossi, the largest in Egypt or Nubia, except the great sphinx at the pyramids, to which they approach in the proportion of nearly two thirds. From the shoulder to the elbow they measure fifteen feet six inches; the ears three feet six inches; the face seven feet; the beard five feet six inches; across the shoulders twenty-five feet four inches; their height is about fifty-one feet, not including the caps, which are about fourteen feet.

One of the Enormous Sitting Colossi.

"There are only two of these colossi in sight: one is still buried under the sand, and the other, which is near the door, is half fallen down, and buried also. On the top of the door is a colossal figure of Osiris, twenty feet high, with two colossal hieroglyphic figures, one on each side, looking towards it. On the top of the temple is a cornice with hieroglyphics, a torus and frieze under it. The cornice is six feet wide, the frieze is four feet. Above the cornice is a row of sitting monkeys eight feet high, and six feet wide across the shoulders. They are twenty-one in number. This temple was nearly two-thirds buried under the sand, of which we removed thirty-one feet before we came to the upper part of the door. It must have had a very fine landing-place, which is now totally buried under the sand. It is the last and largest temple excavated in the solid rock in Nubia or Egypt, except the new tomb in Beban el Molook.

"The heat on first entering the temple was so great that they could scarcely bear it, and the perspiration from their hands was so copious as to render the paper, by its dripping, unfit for use. On the first opening that was made by the removal of the sand, the only living object that presented itself was a toad of prodigious size. Halls and chambers, supported by magnificent columns and adorned with beautiful intaglios, paintings, and colossal figures, the walls being covered partly with hieroglyphics, and partly with exhibitions of battles, storming of castles, triumphs over the Ethiopians, sacrifices, &c.— made up the striking interior."

Nothing but the most extraordinary degree of enthusiasm could have supported Belzoni in the numerous descents which he made into the mummy pits of Egypt, and through the long narrow subterraneous passages, particularly inconvenient for a man of his size—for he was six feet and a half in height, and muscular in proportion.

"Of some of these tombs," says he, "many persons could not withstand the suffocating air, which often causes fainting. A vast quantity of dust arises, so fine that it enters the throat and nostrils, and chokes the nose and mouth to such a degree that it requires great power of lungs to resist it and the strong effluvia of the mummies. This is not all; the entry or passage where the bodies are is roughly cut in the rocks, and the falling of the sand from the upper part or ceiling of the passage causes it to be nearly filled up. In some places there is not more than the vacancy of a foot left, which you must contrive to pass through in a creeping posture like a snail, on pointed and keen stones that cut like glass. After getting through these passages, some of them two or three hundred yards long, you generally find a more commodious place, perhaps high enough to sit. But what a place of rest! surrounded by bodies, by heaps of mummies in all directions, which, previous to my being accustomed to the sight, impressed me with horror. The blackness of the wall, the faint light given by the candles or torches for want of air, the different objects that surrounded me seeming to converse with each other, and the Arabs with the candles or torches in their hands, naked and covered with dust, themselves resembling living mummies, absolutely formed a scene that cannot be described. In such a situation I found myself several times, and often returned exhausted and fainting, till at last I became inured to it and indifferent to what I suffered, except from the dust, which never failed to choke my throat and nose; and though, fortunately, I am destitute of the sense of smelling, I could taste that the mummies were rather unpleasant to swallow. After the exertion of entering into such a place, through a passage of fifty, a hundred, three hundred, or perhaps six hundred yards, nearly overcome, I sought a resting-place, found one, and contrived to sit; but when my weight bore on the body of an Egyptian, it crushed it like a band-box. I naturally had recourse to my hands to sustain my weight, but they found no better support, so that I sunk altogether among the broken mummies, with a crash of bones, rags, and wooden cases, which raised such a dust as kept me motionless for a quarter of an hour waiting till it subsided again. I could not remove from the place, however, without increasing it, and every step I took I crushed a mummy in some part or other.

"Once I was conducted from such a place to another resembling it, through a passage of about twenty feet in length, and no wider than that a body could be forced through. It was choked with mummies, and I could not pass without putting my face in contact with that of some decayed Egyptian, but as the passage inclined downwards my own weight helped me on; however, I could not avoid being covered with bones, legs, arms, and heads rolling from above. Thus I proceeded from one cave to another, all full of mummies piled up in various ways, some standing, some lying, and some on their heads. The purpose of my researches was to rob the Egyptians of their papyri, of which I found a few hidden in their breasts, under their arms, in the space above the knees, or on the legs, and covered by the numerous folds of cloth that envelope the mummy. The people of Gournou, who make a trade of antiquities of this sort, are very jealous of strangers, and keep them as secret as possible, deceiving travellers by pretending that they have arrived at the end of the pits when they are scarcely at the entrance. I could never prevail on them to conduct me into these places till this my second voyage, when I succeeded in obtaining admission into any cave where mummies were to be seen."

M. Drovetti, the French consul, had discovered a sarcophagus in a cavern of the mountains of Gournou, but had endeavoured in vain to get it out; he therefore acquainted Belzoni that he would present him with it. This gave occasion to an adventure which possesses much of the interest of romance in the recital. Mr. Belzoni entered the cavern with two Arabs and an interpreter. He thus describes the enterprise:—

"Previous to our entering the cave we took off the greater part of our clothes, and, each having a candle, advanced through a cavity in the rock, which extended a considerable length in the mountain, sometimes pretty high, sometimes very narrow, and without any regularity. In some passages we were obliged to creep on the ground, like crocodiles. I perceived that we were at a great distance from the entrance, and the way was so intricate that I depended entirely on the two Arabs to conduct us out again. At length we arrived at a large space into which many other holes or cavities opened; and after some examination by the two Arabs, we entered one of these, which was very narrow, and continued downward for a long way, through a craggy passage, till we came where two other apertures led to the interior in a horizontal direction. One of the Arabs then said, 'This is the place.' I could not conceive how so large a sarcophagus as had been described to me could have been taken through the aperture which the Arab now pointed out. I had no doubt but these recesses were burial-places, as we continually walked over skulls and other bones; but the sarcophagus could never have entered this recess, for it was so narrow that on my attempt to penetrate it I could not pass.

"One of the Arabs however succeeded, as did my interpreter; and it was agreed that I and the other Arab should wait till they returned. They proceeded evidently to a great distance, for the light disappeared, and only a murmuring sound from their voices could be distinguished as they went on. After a few moments I heard a loud noise, and the interpreter distinctly crying, 'O, my God, I am lost!' After which, a profound silence ensued. I asked my Arab whether he had ever been in that place? He replied, 'Never.' I could not conceive what could have happened, and thought the best plan was to return, to procure help from the other Arabs. Accordingly, I told my man to show me the way out again; but, staring at me like an idiot, he said he did not know the road. I called repeatedly to the interpreter, but received no answer. I watched a long time, but no one returned; and my situation was no very pleasant one. I naturally returned, through the passages by which we had come; and, after some time, I succeeded in reaching the place where, as I mentioned, were many cavities. It was a complete labyrinth, as all these places bore a great resemblance to the one which we first entered. At last, seeing one which appeared to be the right, we proceeded through it a long way; but, by this time, our candles had diminished considerably, and I feared that if we did not get out soon, we should have to remain in the dark. Meantime, it would have been dangerous to put one out to save the other, lest that which was left should, by some accident, be extinguished. At this time we were considerably advanced towards the outside, as we thought; but, to our sorrow, we found the end of that cavity without any outlet.

"Convinced that we were mistaken in our conjecture, we quickly returned towards the place of the various entries, which we strove to regain. But we were then as perplexed as ever, and were both exhausted from the ascents and descents, which we had been obliged to go over. The Arab seated himself, but every moment of delay was dangerous. The only expedient was to put a mark at the place out of which we had just come, and then examine the cavities in succession, by putting also a mark at their entrance, so as to know where we had been. Unfortunately our candles would not last through the whole: however, we began our operations.

"On the second attempt, when passing before a small aperture, I thought I heard the sound of something like the roaring of the sea at a distance. In consequence, I entered this cavity; and, as we advanced, the noise increased, till I could distinctly hear a number of voices all at one time. At last, thank God, we walked out; and to my no small surprise, the first person I saw was my interpreter. How he came to be there I could not conjecture. He told me that, in proceeding with the Arab along the passage below, they came to a pit, which they did not see; that the Arab fell into it, and in falling put out both candles. It was then that he cried out, 'I am lost!' as he thought he also should have fallen into the pit. But on raising his head, he saw, at a great distance, a glimpse of daylight, towards which he advanced, and thus arrived at a small aperture. He then scraped away some loose sand and stones, to widen the place where he came out, and went to give the alarm to the Arabs, who were at the other entrance. Being all concerned for the man who fell to the bottom of the pit, it was their noise that I heard in the cave. The place by which my interpreter got out was instantly widened: and, in the confusion, the Arabs did not regard letting me see that they were acquainted with that entrance, and that it had lately been shut up. I was not long in detecting their scheme. The Arabs had intended to show me the sarcophagus, without letting me see the way by which it might be taken out, and then to stipulate a price for the secret. It was with this view they took me such a way round about."

Of all the discoveries of Belzoni, the most magnificent was that of a new tomb in the Beban el Molook, or Vale of the Tombs of Kings. "I may call this," says the traveller, "a fortunate day, one of the best perhaps of my life: from the pleasure it afforded me of presenting to the world a new and perfect monument of Egyptian antiquity, which can be recorded as superior to any other in point of grandeur, style, and preservation,—appearing as if just finished on the day we entered it; and what I found in it," he adds, "will show its great superiority to all others." Certain indications had convinced him of the existence of a large and unopened sepulchre. Impressed with this idea, he caused the earth to be dug away to the depth of eighteen feet, when the entrance made its appearance. The passage, however, was choked up with large stones, which were with difficulty removed. A long corridor, with a painted ceiling, led to a staircase twenty-three feet long, and nearly nine feet wide. At the bottom was a door, twelve feet high; it opened into a second corridor of the same width, thirty-seven feet long, the sides and ceiling finely sculptured and painted. "The more I saw," he says, "the more I was eager to see." His progress, however, was interrupted at the end of this second corridor by a pit thirty feet deep and twelve wide. Beyond this was perceived a small aperture of about two feet square in the wall, out of which hung a rope reaching probably to the bottom of the well; another rope fastened to a beam of wood stretching across the passage, on this side also, hung into the well. One of these ropes was unquestionably for the purpose of descending on one side of the well, and the other for that of ascending on the opposite side. Both the wood and the rope crumbled to dust on being touched.

By means of two beams, Belzoni contrived to cross this pit or well, and to force a larger opening in the wall, beyond which was discovered a third corridor of the same dimensions as the two former. Those parts of the wood and rope which were on the further side of this wall did not fall to dust, but were in a tolerably good state of preservation, owing, as he supposed, to the dryness of the air in these more distant apartments. The pit, he thought, was intended as a sort of reservoir to receive the wet which might drain through the ground between it and the external entrance.

"The sepulchre was now found to open into a number of chambers of different dimensions, with corridors and staircases. Of the chambers, the first was a beautiful hall, twenty-seven feet six inches by twenty-five feet ten inches, in which were four pillars, each three feet square. At the end of this room I call the Entrance-hall," says the famous discoverer, "is a large door, from which three steps lead down into a chamber with two pillars. This is twenty-eight feet two inches by twenty-five feet six inches. The pillars are three feet ten inches square. I gave it the name of the Drawing-room; for it is covered with figures, which, though only outlined, are so fine and perfect, that you would think they had been drawn only the day before. Returning into the Entrance-hall, we saw on the left of the aperture a large staircase, which descended into a corridor. It is thirteen feet four inches long, seven and a half wide, and has eighteen steps. At the bottom we entered a beautiful corridor, thirty-six feet six inches by six feet eleven inches. We perceived that the paintings became more perfect as we advanced farther into the interior. They retained their gloss, or a kind of varnish over the colours, which had a beautiful effect. The figures are painted on a white ground. At the end of this corridor we descended ten steps, which I call the small stairs, into another, seventeen feet two inches by ten feet five inches. From this we entered a small chamber, twenty feet four inches by thirteen feet eight inches, to which

I gave the name of the Room of Beauties; for it is adorned with the most beautiful figures in basso relievo, like all the rest, and painted. When standing in the centre of this chamber, the traveller is surrounded by an assembly of Egyptian gods and goddesses.

"Proceeding further, we entered a large hall, twenty-seven feet nine inches by twenty-six feet ten inches. In this hall are two rows of square pillars, three on each side of the entrance, forming a line with the corridors. At each side of this hall is a small chamber. This hall I termed the Hall of Pillars: the chamber on the right Isis' Room, as in it a large cow is painted: that on the left, the Room of Mysteries, from the mysterious figures it exhibits. At the end of this hall we entered a large saloon with an arched roof or ceiling, which is separated from the Hall of Pillars only by a step, so that the two may be reckoned one.

Temple of Isis.

"The saloon is thirty-one feet ten inches by twenty-seven feet. On the right of the saloon is a small chamber without anything in it, roughly cut, as if unfinished, and without painting: on the left we entered a chamber with two square pillars, twenty-five feet eight inches by twenty-two feet ten inches. This I called the Sideboard Room, as it has a projection of three feet in a form of a sideboard all round, which was perhaps intended to contain the articles necessary for the funeral ceremony. The pillars are three feet four inches square, and the whole beautifully painted as the rest. At the same end of the room, and facing the Hall of Pillars, we entered by a large door into another chamber with four pillars, one of which is fallen down. This chamber is forty-three feet four inches by seventeen feet six inches; the pillars three feet seven inches square. It is covered with white plaster, where the rock did not cut smoothly, but there is no painting on it. I named it the Bull's, or Apis' Room, as we found the carcase of a bull in it, embalmed with asphaltum; and also, scattered in various places, an immense quantity of small wooden figures of mummies, six or eight inches long, and covered with asphaltum to preserve them. There were some other figures of fine earth baked, coloured blue, and strongly varnished. On each side of the two little rooms were wooden statues standing erect, four feet high, with a circular hollow inside, as if to contain a roll of papyrus, which I have no doubt they did. We found likewise fragments of other statues of wood and of composition.

"But the description of what we found in the centre of the saloon, and which I have reserved till this place, merits the most particular attention, not having its equal in the world, and being such as we had no idea could exist. It is a sarcophagus of the finest oriental alabaster, nine feet five inches long, and three feet seven inches wide. Its thickness is only two inches; and it is transparent when a light is placed inside of it. It is minutely sculptured within and without with several hundred figures, which do not exceed two inches in height, and represent, as I suppose, the whole of the funeral procession and ceremonies relating to the deceased, united with several emblems. I cannot give an adequate idea of this beautiful and invaluable piece of antiquity, and can only say that nothing has been brought into Europe from Egypt that can be compared with it. The cover was not there; it had been taken out, and broken into several pieces, which we found in digging before the first entrance. The sarcophagus was over a staircase in the centre of the saloon, which communicated in a subterraneous passage, leading downwards, three hundred feet in length. At the end of this passage we found a great quantity of bats' dung, which choked it up, so that we could go no further without digging. It was nearly filled up too by the falling in of the upper part."

This sarcophagus is now to be seen in Sir John Soane's Museum, Lincoln's Inn Fields. The sight of it will richly repay the visitor. Copies of the figures on the walls of the tomb are to be seen in the Egyptian rooms of the British Museum, and form not the least striking of its vast collection of curiosities.

Perhaps the most arduous of Belzoni's enterprises was the opening of the second pyramid of Ghiza, known by the name of Cephrenes, as the largest pyramid is known by the name of Cheops. Herodotus, the ancient Greek historian, was informed that this pyramid had no subterranean chambers, and his information being found in latter ages to be generally correct, may be supposed to have operated in preventing that curiosity which prompted the opening of the great pyramid of Cheops by Shaw. Belzoni, however, perceived certain indications of sufficient weight to induce him to make the attempt.

"The opening of this pyramid," says Mr. Salt, the English consul-general, "had long been considered an object of so hopeless a nature that it is difficult to conceive how any person could be found sanguine enough to make the attempt; and even after the discovery, with great labour, of the forced entrance, it required great perseverance in Belzoni, and confidence in his own views, to induce him to continue the operation, when it became evident that the extensive labours of his predecessors in the enterprise had completely failed. The direct manner in which he dug down upon the door affords the most incontestable proof that chance had nothing to do with the discovery itself, of which Belzoni has given a very clear description."

"On my return to Cairo," says he, "I again went to visit the celebrated pyramids of Ghiza; and on viewing that of Cephrenes I could not help reflecting how many travellers of different nations, who had visited this spot, contented themselves with looking at the outside of the pyramid, and went away without inquiring whether any and what chambers exist within it; satisfied, perhaps, with the report of the Egyptian priests, 'that the pyramid of Cheops only contained chambers in its interior.' I then began to consider the possibility of opening this pyramid. The attempt was, perhaps, presumptuous; and the risk of undertaking such an immense work without success deterred me in some degree from the enterprise. I am not certain whether love for antiquity, an ardent curiosity, or ambition, spurred me on most in spite of every obstacle, but I determined at length to commence the operation.

"I set out from Cairo on the 6th of February, 1818, under pretence of going in quest of some antiquities at a village not far off, in order that I might not be disturbed in my work by the people of Cairo. I then repaired to the Kaiya Bey, and asked permission to work at the pyramid of Ghiza, in search of antiquities. He made no objection, but said that he wished to know if there was any ground about the pyramid fit for tillage. I informed him that it was all stones, and at a considerable distance from any tilled ground. He nevertheless persisted in inquiring of the cachef of the province, if there was any good ground near the pyramids; and after receiving the necessary information, granted my request.

"Having thus acquired permission I began my labours on the 10th of February, at a point on the north side, in a vertical section at right angles to that side of the base. I saw many reasons against my beginning there, but certain indications told me that there was an entrance at that spot. I employed sixty labouring men, and began to cut through the mass of stones and cement which had fallen from the upper part of the pyramid; but it was so hard joined together that the men spoiled several of their hatchets in the operation. The stones which had fallen down along with the cement had formed themselves into one solid and almost impenetrable mass. I succeeded, however, in making an opening of fifteen feet wide, and continued working downwards in uncovering the face of the pyramid. This work took up several days, without the least prospect of meeting with anything interesting. Meantime I began to fear that some of the Europeans residing at Cairo might pay a visit to the pyramids, which they do very often, and thus discover my retreat and interrupt my proceedings.

"On the 17th of the same month we had made a considerable advance downwards, when an Arab workman called out, making a great noise, and saying that he had found the entrance. He had discovered a hole in the pyramid into which he could just thrust his arm and a djerid of six feet long. Towards the evening we discovered a larger aperture, about three feet square, which had been closed in irregularly by a hewn stone. This stone I caused to be removed, and then came to an opening larger than the preceding, but filled up with loose stones and sand. This satisfied me that it was not the real but a forced passage, which I found to lead inwards and towards the south. The next day we succeeded in entering fifteen feet from the outside, when we reached a place where the sand and stones began to fall from above. I caused the rubbish to be taken out, but it still continued to fall in great quantities. At last, after some days' labour, I discovered an upper forced entrance, communicating with the outside from above, and which had evidently been cut by some one who was in search of the true passage. Having cleared this passage I perceived another opening below, which apparently ran towards the centre of the pyramid.

"In a few hours I was able to enter this passage, which runs horizontally towards the centre of the pyramid, nearly all choked up with stones and sand. These obstructions I caused to be taken out, and at halfway from the entrance I found a descent, which also had been forced, and which ended at the distance of forty feet. I afterwards continued the work in the horizontal passage above, in hopes that it might lead to the centre; but I was disappointed, and at last was convinced that it ended there, and that to attempt to advance that way would only incur the risk of sacrificing some of my workmen, as it was really astonishing to see how the stones hung suspended over their heads, resting perhaps by a single point; indeed, one of these stones fell, and had nearly killed one of the men. I therefore retired from the forced passage with great regret and disappointment.

"Notwithstanding the discouragements I met with I recommenced my researches on the following day, depending upon my indications. I directed the ground to be cleared away to the eastward of the false entrance; the stones, encrusted and bound together with cement, were equally hard as the former, and we had as many large stones to remove as before. By this time my retreat had been discovered, which occasioned me many interruptions from visitors.

"On February 28, we discovered a block of granite in an inclined direction towards the centre of the pyramid, and I perceived that the inclination was the same as that of the passage of the first pyramid, or that of Cheops; consequently I began to hope that I was near the true entrance. On the 1st of March we observed three large blocks of stone one upon the other, all inclined towards the centre; these large stones we had to remove as well as others much larger, as we advanced, which considerably retarded our approach to the desired spot. I perceived, however, that I was near the true entrance, and, in fact, the next day about noon, on the 2nd of March, was the epoch at which the grand pyramid of Cephrenes was at last opened, after being closed up so many centuries, that it remained an uncertainty whether any interior chambers did or did not exist."

Belzoni then gives a detailed description of the passages leading to the great chamber of the pyramid. "On entering the great chamber," he continues, "I found it to be forty-six feet three inches long, sixteen feet three inches wide, and twenty-three feet six inches high, for the most part cut out of the solid rock (for this chamber was at the bottom of the pyramid) except that part of the roof towards the western end. In the midst we observed a sarcophagus of granite partly buried in the ground to the level of the floor, eight feet long, three feet six inches wide, and two feet three inches deep inside, surrounded by large blocks of granite, being placed apparently to guard it from being taken away, which could not be effected without great labour. The lid of it had been opened; I found in it only a few bones of a human skeleton, which merit preservation as curious relics, they being in all probability those of Cephrenes, the reported builder of the pyramid."

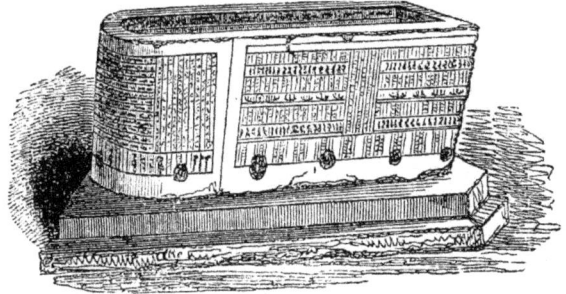

Tomb of Alexander the Great.

It is necessary, however, to inform the young reader that Belzoni, being unversed in osteology, was mistaken here, and that these bones, when examined by scientific men in London, were found to be those of a cow; thus giving foundation for the theory that the bodies of sacred animals, the representatives of the Egyptian gods, were interred with extraordinary honours.

Head of the Great Sphynx.

To narrate all the enterprises of Belzoni would occupy volumes. Let us allude but to one more. He uncovered the front of the great Sphynx—that gigantic monument which has been synonymous with "Mystery" from the remotest ages of history. Numerous pieces of antiquity were as unexpectedly as extraordinarily developed by this enterprise—pieces which, for many centuries, had not been exposed to human eyes. Among other things, a beautiful temple, cut out of one piece of granite, yet of considerable dimensions, was discovered between the legs of the sphynx, having within it a sculptured lion and a small sphynx. In one of the paws of the great sphynx was another temple with a sculptured lion standing on an altar. In front of the great sphynx were the remains of buildings, apparently temples, and several granite slabs with inscriptions cut into them, some entire and others broken. One of these is by Claudius Cæsar, recording his visits to the pyramids, and another by Antoninus Pius, both of which, with the little lions, are now in the British Museum.

Statues at Luxor.

CHAPTER V.

With the progress of civilization, Enterprise took more diversified forms. First, man was summoned to display this commanding quality of mind in the subjugation or destruction of the stronger and fiercer animals; then he had to enter on the perilous adventure into strange regions by land, and the hazardous transit of the ocean, in search of still more unknown countries. We have just glanced at another department of enterprise—the search for antiquities; and the subject was placed in this order because it seemed naturally connected with the perils of travel. But enterprise had taken a thousand forms before men began to venture on great dangers for the attainment of more certain knowledge of the past: the hewing of rocks and levelling of forests, the disembowelling of mines, the construction of highways and harbours, the erection of bridges and lighthouses, of Cyclopæan piles and pyramids, of obelisks and columns, of aqueducts and walls of cities—these, and a thousand other displays of strength, genius, and skill, were among the "Triumphs of Enterprise" ages ago, and they are now succeeded by the formation of railways, and the myriad-fold enterprises of modern science.

How much would we not give for an authentic account of those mysterious enterprises—the building of Stonehenge, of the round towers of Ireland, and of the multitudinous "Druidical" monuments, as they are termed, which are scattered in immense masses over Spain and other parts of the continent? We are left to conjecture for their origin, and our knowledge of it may never reach to certainty. The venerable pyramids themselves are equally mysterious, both as it regards the purposes for which they were erected and the means of erecting them. The Cyclopæan masses of stone which form the foundations of the ruined temple at Balbec (masses which dwarf the stones of the Pyramids), as well as the recently discovered remains in Central America, stretch back into the far past, and also puzzle and confound all human judgment and reckoning.

Stonehenge.

Again, even of some of the more recent erections of antiquity, opinion is divided as to the true cause of carrying out such enterprises. In this predicament antiquarian criticism places the Roman aqueducts—those immense structures, formed often of several miles of arches, on which water was conveyed over valleys. From a passage in Pliny it is argued that the Romans were really acquainted with the hydrostatic truth that water will rise to its own level; that these immense edifices were erected rather from reasons of state policy than from ignorance, the construction of them serving to employ turbulent spirits. All this, however, is doubtful, and it may be that real ignorance stimulated the Romans to carry on and complete these gigantic undertakings which abound in their empire. One, it may be observed, which was begun by Caius Cæsar, but completed by Claudius, and therefore called the Claudian aqueduct, was forty miles in length, and was raised sufficiently to distribute water over the seven hills of the imperial mistress of the world.

Ruins of the Temple at Balbec.

But above all the civil enterprises of the Romans we ought to place their roads; these grand and enduring highways, indeed, stamped Europe with a new feature, and the civilized likeness thus impressed on her was not effaced until railroads gave the initiative to a new civilization. We cannot refrain from quoting Gibbon's masterly description of the Roman highways; it occurs after he has been depicturing the subordinate Roman capitals in Asia Minor, Syria, and Egypt:—"All these cities were connected with each other and with the capital by the public highways, which, issuing from the Forum at Rome, traversed Italy, pervaded the provinces, and were terminated only by the frontiers of the empire. If we carefully trace the distance from the wall of Antoninus (in Scotland) to Rome, and from thence to Jerusalem, it will be found that the great chain of communication from the north-west to the south-east point of the empire was drawn out to the length of 4080 Roman (or 3740 English) miles. The public roads were accurately divided by milestones, and ran in a direct line from one city to another, with very little respect for the obstacles either of nature or private property. Mountains were perforated, and bold arches thrown over the broadest and most rapid streams; the middle part of the road was raised into a terrace which commanded the adjacent country, consisting of several strata of sand, gravel, and cement, and was paved with large stones, or, in some places near the capital, with granite. Such was the solid construction of the Roman highways, whose firmness has not entirely yielded to the effect of fifteen centuries. They united the subjects of the most distant provinces by an easy and familiar intercourse; but their primary object had been to facilitate the marches of the legions, nor was any country considered as completely subdued till it had been rendered in all its parts pervious to the arms and authority of the conqueror. The advantage of receiving the earliest intelligence, and of conveying their orders with celerity, induced the emperors to establish throughout their extensive dominions the regular institution of posts. Houses were everywhere erected at the distance of five or six miles; each of them was constantly provided with forty horses, and by the help of these relays it was easy to travel a hundred miles in a day along the Roman roads. The use of the posts was allowed to those who claimed it by an imperial mandate; but though originally intended for the public service, it was sometimes indulged to the business or conveniency of private citizens."

St. Peter's at Rome.

From other accounts we learn that the Roman roads varied in importance and uses. The great lines were called "Prætorian ways," as being under the direction of the prætors, and those formed the roads for military intercourse. Other lines were exclusively adapted for commerce or civil intercourse, and were under the direction of consuls. Both kinds were formed in a similar manner. The plan on which they were made was more calculated for durability than ease to the traveller, and for our modern wheel carriages they would be found particularly objectionable. Whatever was their entire breadth the centre constituted the beaten track, and was made of large ill-dressed stones laid side by side to form a compact mass of from twelve to twenty feet broad, and therefore in their external aspect they were but coarse stone causeways.

Some of the Roman roads had double lines of this solid pavement, with a smooth brick path for foot passengers, and at intervals along the sides there were elevated stones on which travellers could rest, or from which cavalry could easily mount their horses. One important feature in the construction of all the Roman roads was the bottoming of them with solid materials. Their first operation seems to have been the removal of all loose earth or soft matter which might work upwards to the surface, and then they laid courses of small stones or broken tiles and earthenware, with a course of cement above, and upon that were placed the heavy stones for the causeway; thus a more substantial and durable pavement was formed, the expense being defrayed from the public treasury. Various remains of Roman roads of this kind still exist in France, and also in different parts of Britain. One of the chief Roman thoroughfares, in an oblique direction across the country from London to the western part of Scotland, was long known by the name of Watling Street, and the name has been perpetuated in the appellation of one of the streets of the metropolis.

In the construction of their amphitheatres and other places of public amusement, the Romans far transcended modern nations, in none of which does a theatre exist of dimensions at all comparable with those of the cities in the Roman empire. The ruins of the Colosseum, in Rome itself, are the source of wonder to every visitor. The beautiful lines of Byron on these magnificent remains of Roman civilization are well known.

Respecting numerous other enterprises of the ancient world, interesting but imperfect accounts remain. Such are the narratives of what were termed the "Seven Wonders of the World." It is time, however, to leave antiquity—or, at least, classic antiquity—to speak of one wondrous enterprise—that of a nation at the very "ends of the earth," of whom indeed many wonders are told.

Bell, the enterprising traveller, presents, perhaps, the clearest account of the celebrated "Great Wall of China."

"On the 2nd of November, 1720, about noon," says he, "we could perceive the famous wall, running along the tops of the mountains, towards the north-east. One of our people cried out 'land!' as if we had been all this while at sea. It was now, as nearly as I can compute, about forty English miles from us, and appeared white at this distance. The appearance of it, running from one high rock to another, with square towers at certain intervals, even at this distance is most magnificent."

In two days they arrived at the foot of this mighty barrier, and entered through a great gate into China. Here a thousand men were perpetually on guard, by the officers commanding whom they were received with much politeness, and invited to tea.

"The long, or endless wall, as it is commonly called," continues Bell, "encompasses all the north and west parts of China. It was built about six hundred years ago by one of the emperors, to prevent the frequent incursions of the Mongols and other western Tartars, who made a practice of assembling numerous troops of horse and invading the country in different places. The Chinese frontiers were too extensive to be guarded against such bold and numerous enemies, who, after plundering and destroying a wealthy country, returned to their own loaded with spoils.

"The Chinese, finding all precautions ineffectual to put a stop to the inroads of such barbarians, at last resolved to build this famous wall. It begins in the province of Leotong, at the bottom of the Bay of Nankin, and proceeds across rivers, and over the tops of the highest mountains, without interruption, keeping nearly along the circular ridge of barren rocks that surround the country to the north and west; and, after running southwards about twelve hundred English miles, ends in impassable mountains and sandy deserts.

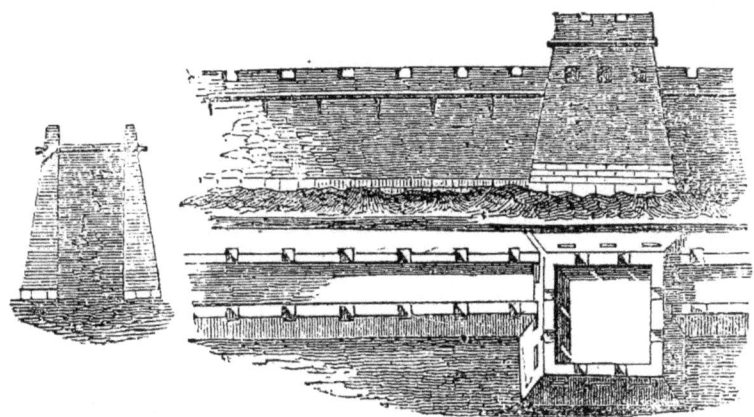

Part of the Great Wall of China.

This is an engraving of a small portion of this wonderful work. At the top is represented a piece of the wall, with one of the towers, as it is seen by a person standing on the ground. Immediately under it is a bird's-eye view of the same, representing the dimensions and position of the tower, in relation to the wall. And on the left side is a section which shows how the masonry is constructed—of two walls getting thinner towards the top, and the intermediate space filled in with work of a rougher kind.

"The foundation consists of large blocks of square stones, laid in mortar; but the rest of the wall is built of brick. The whole is so strong and well built as to need almost no repair, and, in such a dry climate, may remain in this condition for many ages. Its height and breadth are not equal in every place; nor, indeed, is it necessary they should. When carried over steep rocks, where no horse can pass, it is about fifteen or twenty feet high, and broad in proportion; but, when running through a valley, or crossing a river, there you see a strong wall, about thirty feet high, with square towers at the distance of a bow-shot from one another, and embrasures at equal distances. The top of the wall is flat, and paved with broad freestones; and where it rises over a rock, or any eminence, you ascend by a fine easy stone stair. The bridges over rivers and torrents are exceedingly neat, being both well contrived and executed. They have two stories of arches, one above another, to afford sufficient passage for the waters on sudden rains and floods."

Bell was also informed by the Chinese that this wall was completed within the space of five years; every sixth man in the empire having been compelled to work at it, or find a substitute. The date of its erection, however, is considered uncertain; and therefore this account may also be untrue. Gibbon gives the third century before the Christian era as the date of its construction, and assigns it a length of fifteen hundred miles. Du Pauw reduces the length to four hundred and fifty miles, not choosing to consider the western branch, "which," he says, "is of earth, worthy the name of a wall." Many writers judge it to be a very recent work, or, at least, of as modern a date as on this side the thirteenth century, since it is not mentioned by Marco Polo. Yet *tea* is not mentioned by him, although the Chinese have used it for thousands of years. If it be true that much of Marco Polo's manuscript was destroyed because his friends ignorantly believed his wondrous relations (such as the burning of a "black stone," or coal, by the Chinese, for fuel) to be false, the omission of allusions to the Great Wall, in *our* copies of Marco Polo will be no argument against its antiquity.

Next to the Great Wall, the Porcelain Tower of Nankin is usually classed as the great marvel of China. The following curious description of this temple of Boudh, for such the porcelain pagoda is, was purchased in the city of Nankin, on the return of one of our English embassies, and was first published in a leading periodical, which was furnished with a translation by Sir George Staunton, the celebrated scholar and traveller.

"The Dwelling of Security, Tranquillity, and Peace. The representation of the precious glazed tower of the Temple of Gratitude, in the province of Kiang-Nan.

"This work was commenced at noon, on the fifteenth day of the sixth moon, of the tenth year of the Emperor Yong Lo (1413 of the Christian era), of the Dynasty of Ming, and was completed on the first day of the eighth moon, of the sixth year of the Emperor Siuen Té, of the same dynasty, being altogether a period of nineteen years in building.

"The sum of money expended in completing the precious glazed tower was two millions four hundred and eighty-five thousand, four hundred and eighty-four ounces of silver. In the construction of the ornamental globe on the pinnacle of the roof of the tower, forty-eight *kin* (one pound and one-third) in weight of gold (sixty-four pounds), and one thousand four hundred *kin* in weight of copper were consumed. The circumference of this globe is thirty-six *che* (about fourteen inches). Each round or story is eighteen *che* high. In that part of the tower called the quang were consumed four thousand eight hundred and seventy *kin* weight of brass. The iron hoops or rings on the pinnacle of the roof are nine in number, and sixty-three *che* each in circumference. The smaller hoops are twenty-four *che* in circumference, and their total weight is three thousand six hundred *kin*.

"On different parts of the tower are suspended eighty-one iron bells, each bell weighing twelve *kin*, or sixteen pounds. There are also nine iron chains, each of which weighs one hundred and fifty *kin*, and is eighty *che* long. The copper pan with two mouths to it on the roof is estimated to weigh nine hundred *kin*, and is sixty *che* in circumference. There is also a celestial plate on the top weighing four hundred and sixty *kin*, and twenty *che* in circumference. In the upper part of the tower are preserved the following articles:—Of night-illuminating pearls, one string; of water-repelling pearls, one string; of fire-repelling pearls, one string; of dust-repelling pearls, one string; and over all these is a string of Fo's relics. Also an ingot of solid gold, weighing forty *leang* (ounces), and one hundred *kin* weight of tea; of silver, one thousand *leang* weight; of the bright huing, two pieces, weighing one hundred *kin*; of precious stones, one string; of the everlasting physic-money, one thousand strings; of yellow satin, two pieces; of the book hidden in the earth, one copy; of the book of Omitd Fo, one copy; of the book of She Kia Fo, one copy; of the book of Tsie Yin Fo, one copy; all wrapped up together, and preserved in the temple.

"The tower has eight sides or faces, and its circumference is two hundred and forty *che*. The nine stories taken together are two hundred and twenty-eight and a half *che* high. From the highest story to the extreme point of the pinnacle of the roof are one hundred and twenty *che*. The lamps within the tower are seven times seven in number, in all forty-nine lamp-dishes, and on the outside there are one hundred and twenty-eight lamp-dishes. Each night they are supplied with fifty *kin* weight of oil. Their splendour penetrates upwards to the thirty-third heaven—mid-way; they shed a lustre over the people, the good and bad together—downwards; they illuminate the earth as far as the City of Tse Kee Hien, in the Province of Che-Kiang.

"The official title of the head priest of the temple is Chao Sieu. His disciples are called Yue. The total number of priests on the establishment is eight hundred and fifty. The family name of the head mason of the building was Yao, his personal name Sieu, and his native town Tsing Kiang Foo. The family name of the head carpenter was Hoo, his personal name Chung, and his native province Kiang See.

"The extent of the whole enclosure of the temple is seven hundred and seventy *meu* (somewhat less than an English acre) and eight-tenths. To the southward, towards Chin Van San, are two hundred and twenty-six *meu*. Eastward, to the boundary of Chin Sien Seng, are two hundred and thirty-four *meu* and eight-tenths. In the centre is the ground of Hoo Kin Te. Westward, as far as the land of She Hon Hoa, are one hundred and twenty *meu*. And northward, to the land of Lien Sien Song, are one hundred and eighty *meu*.

"Viewing, therefore, this History of the Glazed Tower, may it not be considered as the work of a Divinity? Who shall perform the like?

"Lately, on the fifteenth day of the fifth moon, of the fifth year of Kia King, at four in the morning, the God of Thunder, in his pursuit of a monstrous dragon, followed it into this temple, struck three of the sides of the fabric, and materially damaged the ninth story; but the strength and majesty of the God of the temple are most potent, and the laws of Fo are not subject to change. The tower, by his influence, was therefore saved from entire destruction. The Viceroy and the Foo-Yen reported the circumstance to his imperial majesty; and, on the sixth day of the second moon of the seventh year, the restoration of the damaged parts was commenced, and on the nineteenth day of the fifth moon the repairs were completed.

"On the twenty-ninth day of the sixth moon of the twelfth year of his present majesty, at four in the afternoon, on a sudden there fell a heavy shower of rain, and the God of Thunder again rushed forth in front of the tower, and, penetrating the roof, pursued the great dragon from the top to the bottom. The glazed porcelain tiles of the sixth story were much damaged, and where the God of Thunder issued out at the great gate several of the boards taken from the wood of the heavenly flower-tree were broken. Thus, the God of Thunder, having finally driven away the monstrous dragon, returned to his place in the heavens.

"The priests of the temple reported the event to the local authorities, and the officer Hen submitted the report to his Imperial Majesty, and awaited the issue of the sums required to defray the charge of the repairs. The gates of the tower have been closed for a year while the interior has been repairing.

"'Deny not the presence of a God—a God there is;

He sounds his dread thunder, and all the world trembles.'"

Such is the singular register of the Porcelain Pagoda at Nankin. The terraced mountains have been often mentioned as another wonder of China; but recent travellers declare that these enterprises are exceedingly few in the "flowery" land.

To revert to Europe; the great difficulty is to select the themes of Enterprise. Here is one, however, of a somewhat rude, but yet highly adventurous, and also highly useful kind. It is a sketch of a Swiss wonder—the famous "Slide of Alpnach."

For many centuries the rugged flanks and deep gorges of Mount Pilatus were covered by impenetrable forests; lofty precipices encircled them on all sides. Even the daring hunters were scarcely able to reach them, and the inhabitants of the valley never conceived the idea of disturbing them with the axe. These immense forests were therefore allowed to grow and perish, the most intelligent and skilful considering it quite impracticable to avail themselves of such inaccessible stores.

In November, 1816, Mr. John Rulph, of Rentingen, and three other Swiss gentlemen, entertaining more sanguine hopes, drew up a plan of a slide, founded on trigonometrical measurements; and, having purchased a certain extent of the forests from the commune of Alpnach for 6000 crowns, began the construction of it.

The slide of Alpnach was formed of about 25,000 large pine trees, deprived of their bark, and united together without the aid of iron. It occupied about one hundred and sixty workmen during eighteen months, and cost nearly one hundred thousand francs, or 4166*l.* It was about three leagues, or 44,000 English feet long, and terminated in the Lake of Lucerne. It had the form of a trough about six feet broad, and from three to six deep. Its bottom was formed of three trees, the middle one of which had a groove cut out in the direction of its length, for receiving small rills of water for the purpose of diminishing the friction. The whole slide was sustained by about two thousand supports, and in many places was attached in a very ingenious manner to the rugged precipices of granite. The direction of the slide was sometimes straight and sometimes zigzag, with an inclination of from ten to eighteen degrees. It was often carried along the sides of precipitous rocks, and sometimes over their summits; occasionally it passed underground, and at other times over the deep gorges by scaffoldings one hundred and twenty feet high.

Before any step could be taken in its erection it was necessary to cut several thousand trees to obtain a passage through the impenetrable thickets; and as the workmen advanced, men were posted at certain distances in order to point out the road for their return. Mr. Rulph was often obliged to be suspended by cords, in order to descend precipices many hundred feet high, to give directions, having scarcely two good carpenters among his men, they having been hired as the occasion offered.

All difficulties being at length surmounted, the larger pines, which were about one hundred feet long, and ten inches thick at their smaller extremity, ran through the space of *three leagues*, or *nearly nine miles*, in *three minutes and a half*; and, during their descent, appeared to be only a few feet in length. The arrangements were extremely simple. Men were posted at regular distances along the slide, and as soon as everything was ready the man at the bottom called out to the next one above him, "*Lachez!*"—Let go! The cry was repeated, and reached the top of the slide in three minutes; the man at the top of the slide then cried out to the one below, "*Il vient!*"—It comes! As soon as the tree had reached the bottom, and plunged into the lake, the cry of "*Lachez!*" was repeated as before. By these means a tree descended every five or six minutes. When a tree, by accident, escaped from the trough of the slide, it often penetrated by its thickest extremity from eighteen to twenty-four feet into the earth, and if it struck another tree, it cleft it with the rapidity of lightning.

Such was the enterprising work undertaken and executed under the direction of a single individual. This wondrous structure, however, no longer exists, and scarcely a tree is to be seen on the flanks of Mount Pilatus. Political events having taken away the demand for timber, and another market having been found, the operation of cutting and transporting the trees necessarily ceased.

Let us now glance at the enterprise of erecting a more durable monument. Russia, proud of her Czar, the celebrated Peter the Great, wished to erect a monument to his memory. Catherine the Second was the monarch who had the direction of the work, and her choice for an artist fell upon M. Falconet, who, in his conception of an equestrian statue, resolved that the subordinate parts should bear an equal impress of genius. "The pedestals in general use," he observed, "had no distinctive feature, and adapt themselves equally well to any subject. Being of so universal application they suggest no new or elevated thoughts to the beholder." Falconet wished to make the Czar appear as the father and legislator of his people—great and extraordinary in everything—undertaking and completing that which others were unable to imagine. To carry out this conception a precipitous rock was fixed on for the pedestal, on which the statue should appear with characteristics distinguishing it from those erected to other sovereigns.

Falconet's first idea was to form this pedestal of six masses of rock, bound together with bars of iron or copper; but the objection was urged, that the natural decay of the bands would cause a disruption of the various parts, and present a ruinous aspect, while it would be difficult to insure perfect uniformity in the quality and appearance of the different blocks. The next proposal was to form it of one whole rock; but this appeared impossible, and in a report to the senate it was stated that the expense would be so enormous as almost to justify the abandonment of the undertaking. At length it was resolved to bring to the city of St. Petersburg the largest rock that could be found, cost what it might.

The search for a huge mass of rock was begun, but the whole summer was passed in vain exploration. The idea of forming the pedestal of several pieces had again been entertained, when an immense stone was discovered near Cronstadt, which it was determined to use as the principal mass. Various mechanics having been applied to, refused to undertake the task of removing this stone, as did likewise the Russian Admiralty.

Fortunately for M. Falconet, he was acquainted with a native of Cephalonia, who had assumed the name of Lascary, and who, while serving in the corps of cadets, had given high proofs of mechanic skill. Lascary had all along strenuously recommended the adoption of the original design, and now undertook the formation of the pedestal. A few days after his appointment to this commission he received information from a peasant of a large rock lying in a marsh near a bay in the Gulf of Finland, about twenty miles from St. Petersburg by water. The stone was examined, and the base, by sounding around it, was found to be flat. It was a parallelopipedon in form, and was forty-two feet long, twenty-seven feet wide, and twenty-one feet high. These were dimensions sufficiently extensive to realise the conceptions of M. Falconet. The authorities, when the mass was beheld, again recommended its being cut into separate portions for convenient removal. The Empress Catherine and her minister Betzky, were, however, on the side of Lascary, and orders were imperatively given to commence the strange enterprise.

The resolution was taken by M. Lascary to remove the stone without the use of rollers, as these not only present a long surface, which increases the friction and thereby impedes speed, but are not easily made of the great diameter that would have been required owing to the soft and yielding nature of the ground on which the work was to be performed. Spherical bodies, revolving in a metallic groove, were then chosen as the means of transport. These offered many advantages; their motion is more prompt than that of rollers, with a less degree of friction, as they present but small points of contact. Beams of wood, of a foot square, and thirty-three feet in length, were then prepared; one side was hollowed in the form of a gutter, and lined, the sides being convex to the thickness of two inches, with a composition of copper and tin. Balls of the same composite metal, five inches in diameter, were then made, to bear only on the bottom of the groove. These beams were intended to be placed on the ground in a line in front of the stone, while upon them were reversed two other beams prepared in a similar manner, each forty-two feet long and one foot and a half square, connected as a frame by stretchers and bars of iron fourteen feet in length, carefully secured by nuts, screws, and bolts.

A load of three thousand pounds, when placed on the working model (which had been first constructed) was found to move with ease. Betzky, the minister, was pleased with the exhibition of the model; but the crowds who came to witness it cried, "A mountain upon eggs!" But Lascary was not to be driven from his purpose, so intelligently formed, by a little unthinking clamour.

The rock lay in a wild and deserted part of the country, and therefore the first thing to be done was to build barracks capable of accommodating four hundred labourers, artisans, and others. These, with M. Lascary, were all lodged on the spot, as the readiest means of forwarding the work. From the rock to the river Neva a line of road was then cleared a distance of six versts, or twenty-one thousand English feet, to a width of one hundred and twenty feet, in order to gain space for the various operations and to give a free circulation of air, so essential to the health of workmen in a marshy district, as well as to the drying and freezing of the ground—a point of much importance when the enormous weight to be removed is considered. The operation of disinterring the rock was commenced in December, when the influence of the frosts began to be felt. It was embedded to the depth of fifteen feet; the excavation required to be of great width—eighty-four feet all round—to admit of turning the stone, which did not lie in the most favourable position for removal. An inclined plane, six hundred feet in length, was afterwards made, by means of which, when the stone was turned, it might be drawn up to the level surface.

Objectors said it would be impossible to place the monster mass of rock upon the machine destined to transport it; but Lascary was still unshaken. Preferring simplicity to complication, he resolved to employ ordinary levers, known technically as levers of the first order. These were made of three masts, each sixty-five feet in length, and a foot and a half in diameter at the larger end, firmly bound together. To lessen the difficulty of moving these, triangles of thirty feet high were erected, with windlasses attached near the base, from which a cord, passing through a pulley at the top, was fastened to the smaller end of the lever, which being drawn up to the top of the triangle, was ready for the operation of turning; each of these levers was calculated to raise a weight of two hundred thousand pounds.

A row of piles had been driven into the ground at the proper distance from the stone on one side, to serve as a fulcrum; and on the other a series of piles were disposed as a platform, to prevent the sinking of the mass on its descent. Twelve levers, with three men to each, were stationed at the side to be lifted, and the lower extremities being placed under the mass, the upper ends were drawn downwards by the united action of the twelve windlasses. When the stone rose to the height of a foot, beams and wedges were then driven underneath to maintain it in that position, while the levers were arranged for a second lift. To assist the action of the levers, large iron rings were soldered into the upper corner of the rock, from which small cables were passed to four capstans, each turned by thirty-six men, thus maintaining a steady strain, while the stone was prevented from returning to its original position when the levers were shifted. These operations were repeated until the rock was raised nearly to an equipoise, when cables from six other capstans were attached to the opposite side, to guard against a too sudden descent; and as a further precaution against fracture, a bed six feet in thickness, of hay and moss intermingled, was placed to receive the rock, on which it was at length happily laid. As it was of great importance that all the workmen should act at one and the same time, two drummers were stationed on the top of the stone, who, at a sign from the engineer, gave the necessary signals on their drums, and secured the certainty of order and precision in the various operations.

The machinery for the removal had, in the meantime, been finished. Of the lower grooved beams already described, six pairs were prepared, so that when the rock had advanced over one pair they might be drawn forward and placed in a line in advance of the foremost, without interrupting the movements. The balls were laid in the grooves two feet apart; the upper frame, intended as the bed for the rock, placed above. The mass, weighing in its original form four millions of pounds, or nearly eighteen hundred tons, was then raised by means of powerful screws, and deposited on the frame, when it was drawn up the inclined plane by the united force of six capstans. The road did not proceed in a direct line to the river, owing to the soft state of portions of the marsh. It was impossible in many places to reach a firm foundation with piles fifty feet in length. This naturally added to the difficulties of the transport, as the direction of the draught had frequently to be changed. Piles were driven along the whole line on both sides, at distances of three hundred feet apart; to these the cables were made fast, while the capstans revolved, two of which were found sufficient to draw the stone on a level surface, while on unequal ground four were required. From five hundred to twelve hundred feet were got over daily, which, when regard is had to the short winter days of five hours in that high latitude, may be considered as rapid.

So interesting was the spectacle of the enormous mass when moving, with the two drummers at their posts, the forge erected on it continually at work, and forty workmen constantly employed in reducing it to a regular form, that the empress and the court visited the spot to see the novel sight; and notwithstanding the rigour of the season, crowds of persons of all ranks went out every day as spectators. Small flat sledges were attached to each side of the stone by ropes, on which were seated men provided with iron levers, whose duty it was to prevent the balls, of which fifteen on a side were used, from striking against each other and thus impeding the motion. The tool-house was also attached, and moved with the stone, in order that everything might be ready to hand when wanted. Balls and grooves of cast-iron were tried, but this material crumbled into fragments as readily as if made with clay. No metal was found to bear the weight so well as the mixture of copper and tin, and even with this the balls were sometimes flattened and the grooves curled up when the pressure by any accident became unequal. The utility of rollers was also tried; but with double the number of capstans and the power, the cables broke, while the stone did not advance one inch.

Suddenly the enterprise was checked by the sinking of the stone to a depth of eighteen inches in the road, to the chagrin of the engineer, who was suffering under a severe attack of marsh fever. Lascary, however, was not disheartened, and speedily remedied the accident, spite of the idle clamours of the multitude; and in six weeks from the time of first drawing the stone from its bed, he had the satisfaction of seeing it safely deposited on the temporary wharf built for the purpose of embarkation on the banks of the river, when the charge fell into the hands of the Admiralty, who had undertaken the transport by water to the city.

The Russian Admiralty had ordered a vessel or barge one hundred and eighty feet in length, sixty-six feet in width, and seventeen feet from deck to keel, to be built, with every appliance that skill could suggest to render it capable of supporting the enormous burthen. Great precautions were now necessary to prevent the rock falling into the stream. Water was let into the vessel until she sank to the bottom of the river, which brought her deck on a level with the wharf; the rock was then drawn on board by means of two capstans placed on the deck of another vessel anchored at some distance from the shore. Pumps and buckets were now brought into use to clear the barge of the water with which she had been filled; but, to the surprise and consternation of those engaged, she did not rise equally; the centres bearing most of the weight remained at the bottom, while the head and stern springing up gave to the whole the form of a sharp curve; the timbers gave way, and, the seams opening, the water re-entered rapidly; four hundred men were then set to bale, in order that every part might be simultaneously cleared; but the curve became greater in proportion to the diminution of the internal volume of water.

Lascary, who, from the time the rock had been placed on the deck of the vessel, had been a simple spectator of these operations, which occupied two weeks, now received orders to draw it again upon the wharf. He immediately applied himself to remedy the error, which had been committed in not distributing the weight equally, without removing the stone. He first caused the head and stern of the barge to be loaded with large stones, until they sank to a level with the centre; the rock was then raised by means of screws and beams of timber, diverging to every part of the vessel, placed under and against it, and, on the removal of the screws, the pressure being equal in every part, she regained her original form. The water was next pumped out, the stones removed from the head and stern, and a ship lashed on each side of the barge, which on the 22nd of September, 1769, arrived opposite the quay where it was intended to erect the statue. The rock was raised from the spot where it was first found at the end of March preceding.

The debarkation—not the least hazardous part of the enterprise—had yet to be accomplished. As the river was here of a greater depth than at the place of embarkation, rows of piles had been driven into the bottom alongside the quay, and cut off level at a distance of eight feet below the surface. On these the barge was rested; to prevent the recurrence of the rising of the head and stern when the supports should be removed, three masts lashed together, crossing the deck at each extremity, were secured to the surface of the quay. It was then feared that, as the rock approached the shore, the vessel might heel and precipitate it into the river. This was obviated by fixing six other masts to the quay, which projected across the whole breadth of the deck, and were made fast to a vessel moored outside, thus presenting a counterpoise to the weight of the stone. The grooved beams were laid ready, the cables secured, and, at the moment of removing the last support, the drummers beat the signal, the men at the capstans ran round with a cheer, the barge heeled slightly, which accelerated the movement, and in an instant the rock was safety landed on the quay.

The whole expense of the removal of this gigantic rock was about 70,000 roubles, or 14,000*l.*, while the materials which remained were worth two-thirds of the sum.

Dr. Granville, in his "Travels to St. Petersburg," describing the public promenade in front of the Admiralty in that city, says, "Here the colossal equestrian statue of the founder of this magnificent city, placed on a granite rock, seems to command the undivided attention of the stranger. On approaching the rock, the simple inscription fixed on it in bronze letters, 'Petro Primo, Catherina Secunda, MDCCLXXXII,' meets the eye. The same inscription in the Russian language appears on the opposite side. The area is inclosed within a handsome railing placed between granite pillars. The idea of Falconet, the French architect, commissioned to erect an equestrian statue to the extraordinary man at whose command a few scattered huts of fishermen were converted into palaces, was to represent the hero as conquering, by enterprise and personal courage, difficulties almost insurmountable. This the artist imagined might be properly represented by placing Peter on a fiery steed which he is supposed to have taught by skill, management, and perseverance, to rush up a steep and precipitous rock, to the very brink of the precipice, over which the animal and the imperial rider pause, without fear, and in an attitude of triumph. The horse rears with his fore-feet in the air, and seems to be impatient of restraint, while the sovereign, turned towards the island, surveys with calm and serene countenance his capital rising out of the waters, over which he extends the hand of protection. The bold manner in which the group has been made to rest on the hind legs of the horse only, is not more surprising than the skill with which advantage is taken of the allegorical figure of the serpent of envy spurned by the horse, to assist in upholding so gigantic a mass. This monument of bronze is said to have been cast at a single jet. The head was modelled by Mademoiselle Calot, a female artist of great merit, a contemporary of Falconet, and is admitted to be a strong resemblance of Peter the Great. The height of the figure of the emperor is eleven feet; that of the horse seventeen feet. The bronze is in the thinnest parts the fourth of an inch only, and one inch in the thickest part; the general weight of metal in the group is equal to 36,636 English pounds. I heard a venerable Russian nobleman, who was living at St. Petersburg when this monument was in progress, relate that as soon as the artist had formed his conception of the design he communicated it to the empress, together with the impossibility of representing to nature so striking a position of man and animal, without having before his eyes a horse and rider in the attitude he had devised. General Melissino, an officer having the reputation of being the most expert as well as boldest rider of the day, to whom the difficulties of the architect were made known, offered to ride daily one of Count Alexis Orloff's best Arabians out of that nobleman's stud, to the summit of a steep artificial mound formed for the purpose, accustoming the horse to gallop up to it and to halt suddenly, with his fore-legs raised, pawing the air over the brink of a precipice. This dangerous experiment was carried into effect by the general for some days, in the presence of several spectators, and of Falconet, who sketched the various movements and parts of the groups from day to day, and was thus enabled to produce perhaps the finest—certainly the most correct—statue of the kind in Europe."

It thus appears that *enterprise* characterised not only Lascary, the engineer, but Falconet, the artist, Melissino, the officer who undertook to depict the living model, and in brief, the entire deed from beginning to end. How strikingly might the parallel be continued with Peter himself! The young reader will find the history of the Czar, which he can peruse in various forms, pregnant with lessons of enterprise to a degree beyond that of any modern man, with the exception of Napoleon. In both their histories, however, we are compelled to remind him, there is much to censure; and in the history of the latter especially, much more to censure than to praise.

If our own country be viewed with strictness, it will be found that we have no great work of ornamental enterprise simply, at all comparable to the one just sketched. Russia, nevertheless, can bear no comparison with England in point of useful enterprises; she has nothing, for instance, like the Eddystone light-house or the Plymouth breakwater. A few brief sentences will serve to sketch the former.

The first light-house built on the Eddystone rock was constructed by Winstanley, in 1696 to 1700. While some repairs were making under his inspection, the building was blown down in a terrible hurricane, during the night of the 26th of November, 1703, and he and his workmen perished. Not a vestige, except some iron stanchions and a chain, was left behind.

Rudyerd, in 1706, erected another, which was destroyed by fire, in 1755; it was entirely of wood, except the five lower courses of stone, on the rock.

The present edifice is a circular tower of stone sweeping up with a gentle curve from the base, and gradually diminishing to the top, somewhat similar to the swelling of the trunk of a tree. The tower is furnished with a door and windows, and a staircase and ladders for ascending to the lantern, through the apartments of those who keep watch. Mr. Smeaton undertook the arduous task of constructing the present light-house, in the spring of 1756, and completed it in about three years. In order to form his foundation, Smeaton accurately measured the very irregular surface of the rock, and made a model of it. Granite partially worked, forms the foundation; every outside piece is grafted into the rock, to sustain more effectually the action of the sea; a border of three inches effects also a kind of socket for the foundation. Each course of masonry is dovetailed together, in the most skilful manner, and each layer of masonry is strongly cemented together and connected by oaken plugs, and the whole strongly cramped. The general weight of the stones employed is a ton, and some few are two tons. In the solid work the centre stones were fixed first, and all the courses were fitted on a platform and accurately adjusted before they were removed to the rock.

The base of the tower is about twenty-six feet nine inches in diameter; the diameter at the top of the solid masonry is about nineteen feet nine inches; and the height of the solid masonry is thirteen feet from the foundation. The height of the tower from the centre of the base is sixty-one feet seven inches; the lantern, the base of which is stone, is twenty-four feet. The whole height is eighty-five feet seven inches; and the Eddystone light-house has not only the merit of utility, but also of beauty, strength, and originality, and is itself sufficient to immortalise the name of the architect.

The Breakwater thrown across Plymouth Sound is another of the great useful enterprises of Britain. Mr. Rennie was the distinguished engineer appointed to perform this work. He knew that to resist the force of the heavy sea which rolls into the Sound from the south and south-west, a very considerable slope would be necessary for the breakwater, and accordingly, it is so constructed. He also perceived that great masses of stones from one to ten tons each would be required.

The quarries from which these were procured are situated at Oreston on the eastern shore of Catwater; they lie under a surface of about twenty-five acres, and were purchased from the Duke of Bedford for £10,000. They consist of one vast mass of compact close-grained marble, many specimens of which are beautifully variegated; seams of clay, however, are interspersed through the rock, in which there are large cavities, some empty, and others partially filled with clay. In one of these caverns in the solid rock, fifteen feet wide, forty-five feet long, and twelve feet deep, filled nearly with compact clay, were found imbedded fossil bones belonging to the rhinoceros, being portions of the skeletons of three different animals, all of them in the most perfect state of preservation, every part of their surface being entire to a degree which Sir Everard Home said he had never observed in specimens of that kind before. The part of the cavity in which these bones were found was seventy feet below the surface of the solid rock, sixty feet horizontally from the edge of the cliff where it was first begun to work the quarry, and one hundred and sixty feet from the original edge of the Catwater. Every side of the cavern was solid rock, the inside had no incrustation of stalactite, nor was there any external communication through the rock in which it was imbedded, nor any appearance of an opening from above being closed by infiltration. When, therefore, and in what manner these bones came into that situation, is among the secret and wonderful operations of nature which will probably never be revealed to mankind.

M. Dupin, an intelligent observer of our great naval and commercial enterprises gives the following description of the working of the quarries from which the Breakwater stone was procured.

"The sight of the operations which I have just described, those enormous masses of marble that the quarry-men strike with heavy strokes of their hammers; and those aerial roads or flying bridges which serve for the removal of the superstratum of earth; those lines of cranes all at work at the same moment; the trucks all in motion; the arrival, the loading, and the departure of the vessels; all this forms one of the most imposing sights that can strike a friend to the great works of art. At fixed hours, the sound of a bell is heard in order to announce the blastings of the quarry. The operations instantly cease on all sides, the workmen retire; all becomes silence and solitude; this universal silence renders still more imposing the sound of the explosion, the splitting of the rocks, their ponderous fall, and the prolonged sound of the echoes."

These huge blocks of stone were conveyed from the quarries on trucks, along iron railways, to the quays, and from thence into the holds of the vessels built expressly for the purpose. On their arrival over the line of the Breakwater, they are discharged from the trucks by means of what is called a *typing-frame*, at the stern of the vessel, which, falling like a trap-door, lets the stone into the sea. In this manner a cargo of sixteen trucks, or eighteen tons, may be discharged in the space of forty or fifty minutes. Two millions of tons of stone, and one million sterling in money, was the calculation made at the outset, as requisite to complete this great national work.

CONCLUSION.

To describe, even by a single sentence each, the great enterprises of England—her harbours, bridges, canals, railways, mines, manufactures, shipping—would occupy volumes. Suffice it to say that our country has become more and more the land of Enterprise. This, indeed, must be the grand characteristic of the civilised world, universally, if the old and evil passion for war be not renewed.

In bygone ages the only path to prosperity for nations was supposed to be war. Nations seemed to think that without military "glory" they could not be great. Modern nations patterned by the ancient; every page of modern history, as well as ancient, is tilled with battles and successes. The farther we look back, the more we find it true, that violence led to splendour and renown. Much is told of the magnificence of the Eastern empires; but far above the glory of the temples of Tadmor, and the gardens of Babylon, rises the glory of Eastern conquerors on the page of history. Of all that is recorded of Egyptian labour and Corinthian wealth, nothing equals in fame their contemporary warriors. The trade and merchants of Athens were not without profit to her; but to Marathon and Platæa, to Salamis and Mycale, she owes the admiration which the majority in later ages have paid her. Sparta flourished, though condemned to idleness, except in war and theft. The trade of Carthage fell before the sword of Rome, and not all the wares that heathen nations ever fabricated, gave a twentieth part of the power which the soldiers of the republic won.

Gradually, the truth dawns upon the world that war is an evil immeasurable; that military glory is a false and destructive light; and that the grandest enterprises are those which serve to increase the comfort, happiness, and knowledge of the race. Let the young reader bid success to such enterprises, and enter into their spirit with all his energy. To be engaged—to be busy— to be earnestly at work, he will find to be one of the chief sources of happiness; and to pass life honourably and worthily, it is not only the duty, but the privilege, of well-nigh every native of our own and other civilised countries, to render existence a series of the "TRIUMPHS OF ENTERPRISE."